DUNSTABLE:

Its History and Surroundings.

By WORTHINGTON G. SMITH,

F.L.S., F.A.I., F.R.S.A., Ireland.

First Freeman of Dunstable.

ILLUSTRATED WITH DRAWINGS BY THE AUTHOR
AND BY PHOTOGRAPHS.

PUBLISHED BY THE HOMELAND ASSOCIATION FOR THE
ENCOURAGEMENT OF TOURING IN GREAT BRITAIN,
IN CO-OPERATION WITH THE CORPORATION OF DUNSTABLE.

LONDON : Elliot Stock, 62, Paternoster Row.
DUNSTABLE : Miles Taylor, The Gazette Office.
THE HOMELAND ASSOCIATION, LTD. : 22, Bride Lane,
Fleet Street, E.C.

———

1904.

A

CONTENTS.

TO

MY TWO SONS,

ARTHUR AND EDWARD

AND

MY DAUGHTER

EDITH.

LIST OF ILLUSTRATIONS.

PREFACE.

THE idea of this volume originated with my friend Mr. James Field, Councillor of the Borough of Dunstable. Mr. Field put myself in communication with the Home-land Association, whose useful work in the interests of British topography is now well known, and a representative local Committee of the Corporation was formed. This Committee unanimously decided to ask the writer of these lines to put the necessary notes together for publication.

The Committee consisted of—
The Mayor—Alderman CHARLES BOSKETT.
The Town Clerk—CHAS. CRICHTON STUART BENNING.
Alderman ARTHUR ED. LANGRIDGE.
Councillor ARTHUR W. NASH,
    ,,   WILLIAM C. WOOD,
    ,,   EDWARD FRANKLIN,
    ,,   CHAS. D. LOCKHART,
    ,,   ALFRED J. WARREN,
    ,,   JAMES FIELD, Chairman.

For financial reasons, it was necessary to secure a certain number of local advertisements. The request for these was heartily and loyally responded to. The names of the advertisers are the names of the local men who have really made the production of this book possible. I thank them all.

I have also to thank Mr. C. C. S. Benning, Dr. Augustus Morcom, Mr. L. C. R. Thring, Mr. F. Cartwright, solicitor, Mr. B. Bennett, Mr. A. Inwards, and many other gentlemen of the town, for information, hints, and suggestions. My thanks are also here heartily given to the old village folk of the district, who for many years have given me information about old place-names, old buildings, old paths and roads—now lost—old traditions, and old superstitions. Some of these assistants are mentioned by name in the body of the book.

As for the book itself, its shortcomings are no doubt numerous. Some of the omissions are due to the fact that room could be made for nothing more. The work could easily have been made four or six times its present size. Imperfect as it undoubtedly is, no stranger could have written or compiled it straight off. It really represents the observation, note-taking and reading—almost always under difficult conditions—of very many years.

I like to consider all the folk of Dunstable and its neighbourhood as my friends. All are friends round Dunstable. To these friends, learned and unlearned, well-to-do and poor, I venture to offer this little book.

W. G. S.

23 . 3 . 1904.

Natus 23 . 3 . 1835.

Photograph]   ***West Street, Dunstable.***   *J. Field.*
The ancient Icknield Way.

CHAPTER I.

Introduces Dunstable to the Reader.

DUNSTABLE may be reached by railway by the Great Northern, the Midland, and the London and North-Western. The London & North-Western is circuitous and seldom used, travellers wishing to reach Dunstable by this line from Harrow, Berkhampstead, Tring, etc., must change at Leighton **How to get** Buzzard for the local train to Dunstable. **to Dunstable.** The Midland is frequently used, but passengers must change on to the Great Northern line at Luton where the two lines adjoin. The Great Northern is the direct line for Dunstable, there are nine or ten trains every week-day and two or three on Sunday. The time required for the journey by the railway is from 1 hour 20 minutes to 1 hour 25 minutes. Some of the trains proceed to Dunstable without change of carriage; with others a change is made at Hatfield. Church Street is the station at which to alight by the Great Northern. The North-Western Station is at the extreme north end of the town. The single third class fare to Dunstable is 2s. 1od., first-class, 4s. 4d.; there is no second class.

In travelling on the branch from Hatfield to Dunstable five stations are passed—Ayot, Wheathampstead, Harpenden, Luton Hoo, and Luton. The local trains stop at all these stations.

Dunstable can easily be reached by road from London, the distance is thirty-three miles and the roads **By Road.** are well known to be generally good for bicycle or motor. The direct road from the Post Office is by the *Angel* inn, Islington, and Liverpool Road to the *Nag's Head* inn, Holloway, then under Highgate Archway to Finchley, Barnet, St. Albans, and Dunstable. If it is desired to reach Dunstable by Hatfield, Wheathampstead, and Luton, the distance is thirty-six or thirty-seven miles, and the road to the right must be taken at Barnet, the left leads to St. Albans. If a start is made from the Marble Arch the way is through Edgeware to St. Albans.

Dunstable as a place-name does not occur in Domesday Book, although the villages near by, **Meaning of** even the smallest, find a place. Between **the Modern** the years 1100 and 1120, in the beginning of **Name.** the reign of Henry I, and from fifteen to thirty years before the foundation of Dunstable Priory, Geoffrey, afterwards 16th Abbot of St. Albans, according to Matthew Paris, produced the miracle play of St. Katherine at " Dunestapel." This was very soon after the death of William the Conqueror, therefore it is probable that in the time of William I. there was a small Anglo-Saxon and Norman village of wooden cottages, and possibly a wooden church, where Dunstable now stands. The same spelling Dunestapel occurs in the charter of Henry I., written about 1132. On a thirteenth century seal of the Priory the name is spelt Dunstaple. The name is derived from the Anglo-Saxon,—dun, middle-English,—dune,—a hill, and stapel (latterly staple), —a derived and modified form of the old French estaple,

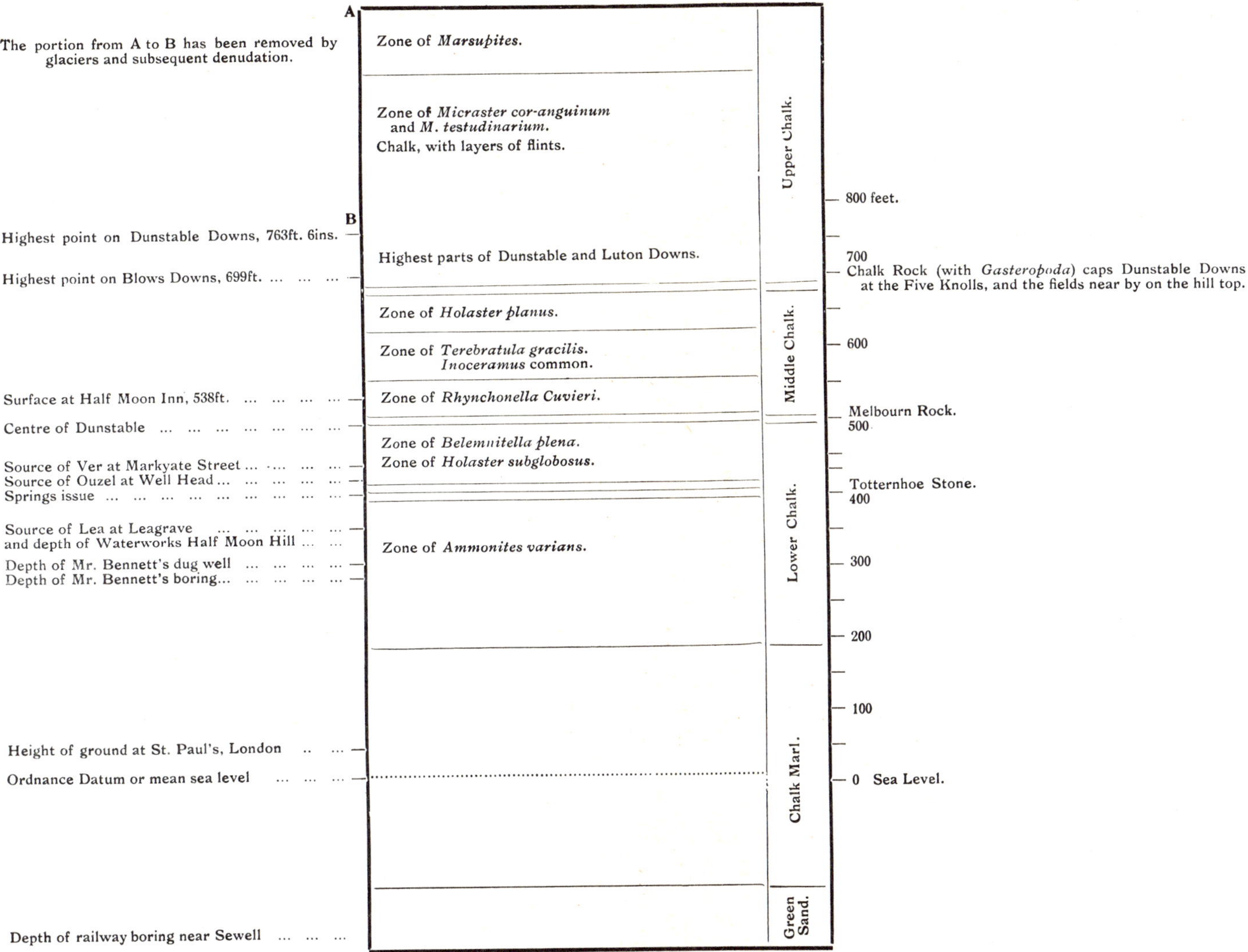

Section for 1,000 feet under the highest part of Dunstable Downs, showing height of Dunstable, the depth of the sources of the Lea, Ouzel and Ver, the depths of the Dunstable Waterworks Wells, Mr. Bennett's Well, the Railway Well sunk near Sewell, with the Zones of Chalk-Rock, Melbourn Rock, Totternhoe Stone, and the Zones of the chief prevailing fossils.

The strata dip 100 feet from the Five Knolls towards Kensworth.

a mart or general market. The name, therefore, means the market place by the hills. The present second syllable stable is a comparatively modern corruption of staple. Old French was in use in the time of Henry I. The lost inscription on his momument in Westminster Abbey was in Norman French, and the same language occurs on tombs close to Dunstable, as at Tilsworth.

Situation. Dunstable is situated in the Hundred of Manshead on the southern border of Bedfordshire, thirty-three miles north-west by north from London and twenty miles south by west from Bedford. The town occupies an important position on the great north road which runs from London to Chester and Holyhead, the road is the ancient Roman road or Watling Street. The town is crossed at right angles in the Market Place by the Icknield Way,—now Church Street and West Street.

Height above Sea Level. The height of Dunstable is 488 feet above the Ordnance datum or horizontal line used in the Ordnance survey, the approximate mean water level at Liverpool. The highest point close to Dunstable is upon Dunstable Downs, near the junction of the Kensworth and Whipsnade Heath roads, where the height is 799 feet 6 inches, the lowest point is in Dunstable Park at 472 feet.

The lowest point in the neighbourhood of Dunstable is at " Well Head," one-and-half miles south-west from the centre of the town, but this low point is really as high above the sea as the cross of St. Paul's Cathedral, London. If the Cathedral could be transported to " Well Head " the cross would just agree in height with the highest point of the closely adjoining Downs. When therefore strollers walk over Dunstable Downs they are elevated in pure bracing air, directly facing the health-giving west wind, at twice the height of St. Paul's Cathedral.

The average rainfall, taken for the past thirty years at Apsley Guise, near Woburn, by E. E. Dymond, Esq., is 24 11 inches per annum.

Photograph]   **Dunstable. High Street (North).**   [II. A. Strange.

The central parts of Dunstable are built upon the rock known to geologists as the upper part of the **The Chalk Downs.** Lower Chalk, the northern parts of the town are built on the Middle Chalk. The chalk is eighty feet deep in the middle of the town and 130 feet deep in the northern parts. Chalk is everywhere in the immediate district. When the stroller stands on Dunstable Downs he has 350 feet of Upper, Middle and Lower Chalk beneath his feet. As the chalk is full of fissures it cannot retain water, consequently the town and hills are always practically dry even after the heaviest and most persistent rainfalls. The chalk of the hills only supports very short herbage and velvet-like turf, it follows therefore that in the wettest weather, wanderers may traverse miles of the breezy downs without getting wet-footed.

Water taken from a river or brook, however near to a spring and however sparkling and apparently **Water Supply.** clear it may be, is never free from dangerous impurities. A brook or river necessarily receives the contaminated washings of fields, farm-yards, and human dwellings. The case of Dunstable is different, the town is supplied with excellent water drawn from two deep wells on Half-Moon hill on the south side of the town. The well is sunk to the base of the Chalk-marl at the bottom of the Lower Chalk, 192 feet from the ground surface on Half-Moon hill. An adjoining boring is carried to down 203 feet, or 98 feet deeper than the source of the river Ouzel at Well-Head. Each well is 8 feet in diameter with extensive headings at the bottom. They are provided with two sets of pumps and the pumping power is equal to 18,000 gallons per hour.

As the Dunstable water is naturally filtered through from 200 to 450 feet of chalk it follows that it flows from the well in a state of high purity and excellent quality free from all contamination and of moderate hardness. The water in the wells varies in depth according to the rainfall of previous months, it has been known to rise 20 feet in a week, it once rose 13 feet in 24 hours. Nearly a year is required for the percolation of the water from the surface to the lowest springs. At Mr. Benjamin Bennett's brewery at the north end of the town, the well is 40 feet below the level of the bottom of the waterworks wells, and even there the bottom of the Lower Chalk is not reached. For brewing purposes the well produces between 30,000 and 40,000 gallons of the purest water per hour.

The air of Dunstable may be said to be highly exhilarating and absolutely pure, no large **The Purity of the Air.** towns contaminate it with smoke and impurities. No smoke-producing factories are anywhere near. The prevailing winds are west and south-west as in other parts of England. When one stands upon Dunstable Downs and looks in a westerly or south-westerly direction only small villages, far apart, can be seen as far as the eye can reach. The villages are 140 feet lower than Dunstable and 450 feet lower than the hill tops. Stagnation of air and smoky town fogs are unknown. ·When the nearest towns are enveloped in smoke and fog, Dunstable is usually enjoying bright sunshine.

The parish of Dunstable is less in size than a mile square and the town practically covers the **Area and Population.** entire parish. The area, according to the Ordnance Survey is 452·572 acres and the valuation list 431 acres. Dunstable ends at Union Street in the north, at the " Half Moon " inn in the south, just short of the railway station in Church Street in the east, at Leighton Gap, or " Boundary Villa " on the north side of West Street, and at the " Rifleman " inn on the south side of the street, in the west. Houses extend for nearly mile beyond the parish boundary on the north, these are in the adjoining parish of Houghton Regis.

The population in 1901 was 5,147—males 2,283, females 2,864.

Dunstable is remarkable for its freedom from infectious diseases, and for the general good health **Health.** and long life of its inhabitants. It is noted for the number of hale old folks always to be seen about. A common age at death is 80 and 90, and sometimes a death is registered at 100 years and even upwards.

Although Dunstable is built on very high ground and is sheltered by grassy chalk hills to the east and west, yet the rainfall is much less than the rainfall of London. The sunshine is of course much more, for when London is sometimes full of suffocating winter fog, the Dunstable hills are usually bathed in sunshine. Storms commonly break up, and do not exhaust themselves over the town ; they have a tendency to expend themselves in the valleys to the east and west.

The healthiness of the town is promoted by its great altitude above the sea level, by its dryness, by the purity of its water and air, by its perfect drainage and the great width of its two main streets. The streets are unusually wide, and in these there are always currents of invigorating fresh air, and at all times more than an average amount of light and sunshine.

Dunstable with its pure bracing air is known to be a highly suitable place for the quick relief of all cases of nervous exhaustion and insomnia.

The death-rate of Dunstable is unusually low, in 1902 **Death-rate.** only 76 deaths occurred, this is equal to a death-rate of only 14·7 per thousand. During the last thirteen years, the lowest death-rate has been 12·1 and the highest 17·9 per thousand. The published returns are as follows :—

1890 ....total 55=12·1	1897 ....total 69=13·5
1891 .... ,, 79=17·2	1898 .... ,, 70=13·1
1892 .... ,, 76=16·8	1899 .... ,, 98=17·9
1893 .... ,, 57=12·5	1900 .... ,, 73=13·3
1894 .... ,, 62=12·76	1901 .... ,, 82=15·9
1895 .... ,, 70=13·76	1902 .... ,, 76=14·7
1896 .... ,, 68=13·7	

For the three months, ending Lady Day, 1903, there were only 12 deaths registered, equal to an annual death-rate of only 9 per thousand. For the adjoining parishes of Houghton Regis, Totternhoe, Kensworth, Whipsnade, and Studham, there were only 3 deaths, equalling an annual death-rate of only 2·9 per thousand.

The whole of the town, except a few small streets in recently developed estates, not yet open to **Drainage of Dunstable.** traffic, was drained in 1891, into a complete system of sewers supplied in various parts of the town with automatic flushing chambers. The outfall site of forty acres is about two miles from the centre of the town on the north-east of the chalk-hill cutting. The sewage is treated by broad irrigation.

The Dunstable Grammar School, or to give it its full title, the Ashton Grammar School, Dunstable, is founded on, and endowed with funds left by Mrs. Francis Ashton in 1728. These funds were originally left as endowment for Almshouses in Dunstable, but the property having increased very greatly in value, the surplus was put by, year by year, until sufficient funds had accumulated to build and endow firstly voluntary schools in Dunstable, and afterwards the Grammar School, the original Almshouses being still maintained.

The Grammar School.

In 1887 the foundation-stone of the School was laid, and the buildings were formally opened on the 27th July 1888. The school house is a handsome building designed by Mr. E. A. Robson, supervising architect to the Educational Department. It has the advantage of all modern school improvements. In addition to the six acres immediately attached to the School, an excellent cricket field has been laid out on land belonging to the School, in the highest part of the town, some three minutes' walk from the School house. In the School grounds are also a Gymnasium, Swimming Bath, Fives Court, Laboratory, Carpenters' Shop, etc.

The School opened in 1888 with three boarders and forty-six day boys; it now has sixty-four boarders and eighty-three day boys. A new boarding house has been added and special arrangements are made for boys coming in daily from Luton. The Head Master is Mr. L. C. R. Thring, M.A.

A high-grade public secondary Girls' School will be immediately established in the town for a hundred scholars, on similar lines with the Ashton Grammar School. The County Council wishes to make Dunstable the centre of secondary education in the southern part of the County, as Bedford is for the northern, and the funds of Chew's Charity being no longer required

Photograph]   **Grammar School, Dunstable.**   [James Field.

for their original purpose, will be devoted to the endowment of the Girls' School which is required to carry out this scheme.

There are Ashton Elementary Schools for boys and girls in connection with the Beds County Council and the Board of Education, Head Master, Mr. Jas. Knight. A scholarship is awarded annually to one boy from this school to the Ashton Grammar School. In the girls' department, the Head Mistress is Miss M. Wilkes. There is a Parochial Infant School, Church Street, Head Mistress, Mrs. Farmer.

There is also a Wesleyan Day School at the rear of the chapel of that religious denomination in the Square. There are two departments—the mixed School, of which Mr. R. Parker Graham is Head Master; the Infant Department is in charge of Miss M. Anderson. This School has about 450 children iu attendance. The School is "Wesleyan" in name only, as nothing in the nature of denominational or sectarian teaching is in the curriculum. There is a County Council—formerly a Board School, in the Chiltern Road in the adjoining parish of Houghton Regis; this is practically in Dunstable. There is a School for Girls in West Street, and a Kindergarten School for young children, under the direction of Miss Herington, in West Street and High Street South. There is also a Day and Boarding School for Girls at Wentworth House, High Street North, conducted by Miss Beaman.

The Town Hall is situated in the centre of the town, **Town Hall.** and replaces an older building burnt down in 1879. It is used on market day (Wednesday) as a Corn Exchange, and sometimes as an Auction Room, it was formerly utilized for the sale of straws and straw plait brought from the villages, but little plaiting is now done. It is also used for public meetings, lectures, concerts, and theatrical entertainments, and sometimes on Sundays for religious services. The Council Chamber is used for meetings of the Town Council, as a Court of Justice, and occasionally for lectures and private meetings. It contains photographs, transcriptions, and translations of the earlier Charters of the town, given by Henry I. and Henry III., from the Public Record Office. A life-size photograph of the bronze effigy of Henry III. from the tomb in Westminster Abbey, photographs of the Great Seals of Henry I. and Henry III. from examples in the British Museum, and photographs and transcriptions of two or three very early Seals belonging to Dunstable Priory from the collection in the British Museum. It also contains portraits of some of the Mayors, and a view of the Market Place drawn in 1885.

The Tudor Arch and Window adjoining the Town Hall. The semicircular stone arch with Doric columns and mullioned window above, probably belongs to the latter part of the sixteenth century, The work is now little more than an external shell, and so many alterations and demolitions have taken place at this spot that it is now impossible to say what the work means. It may have led to the back of a superior house of stone, or have been part of an ancient inn, or first a house and next an inn. The building on the south is the comparatively new town hall; that on the north has only recently been built. The latter replaces an old inn named the "Anchor," but there was a pre-existing inn named the "White Horse." This might have been an altered sixteenth-century house with a small courtyard, afterwards made an inn-yard. Long ago there was a right of way under this arch to West Street named Houghton Lane, a near cut from West Street to Upper Houghton Regis.

Technical Classes. In connection with the Dunstable Technical Education Committee and the Beds County Council, these classes are held in the evenings of the winter months at the Grammar School. Science, Art, Manual, Commercial, and Domestic Subjects are taught.

The town possesses Cricket, Chess, Bowls, Tennis, Unionist and Liberal Clubs. There is is good hunting, and during the winter months the meets are frequently near Dunstable. It is common to see the hounds trotting through the town.

The Gateway of the Old Anchor Inn, Dunstable.

Half a century ago nearly the whole of the Straw
Plait trade was carried on at Dunstable,
The Trades of but it has now been mostly transferred to
the Town. Luton. At this time all the village folk
were more or less straw-plaiters, and the children were
sent to "plaiting-schools" at four years of age. The
best straw was brought from the village of Barton-on-
the-Clay, near Luton, where the corn was reported to be
proof against the discoloring disease termed "rust."
The chief Dunstable firms are Messrs. Munt and Brown,
Woolley Saunders, Stuart and Sons, Taylor Bros.,
Bennett, and Warren. Most of these firms have London
or Luton branches.

There are Lime and Whiting Works in and near the
town, a large manufactory belonging to Messrs. Waterlow
and Sons, of London, and an engineering establishment
carried on by Messrs. Harrison, Carter, and Co.

An attempt is being made to establish a Museum. If
this takes definite form only objects of local
Museum. interest should be accepted. All mere
"curios" and things having nothing to do with Dunstable and its neighbourhood should be respectfully
declined.

CHAPTER II.

The Story of Primeval and Early Man as exemplified in the Dunstable District.

THE most ancient races of men are named Palaeolithic,* because they were the makers of the most ancient implements of stone. Tens of thousands of years have passed since these men lived in England, hundreds of thousands since they lived in some parts of the Eastern Hemisphere. In north-western

Primeval Man and Beast.

Europe there was in times long past a great Glacial Period during which the greater part of England, including Dunstable, was deeply buried under ice and snow. The cause and date of this Glacial Period are unknown, different dates have been given, founded on astronomical and geological observations. Messrs. Adhémar and Croll have placed the period of extreme cold at 800,000 years ago. Towards the close of this Glacial Period, and when the counties south of the Thames were under the sea, the solid ice which covered the Midlands broke up in the form of icebergs, occasionally carrying a bear, a reindeer, or perhaps a Siberian mammoth, and laden with glacially striated boulders and pieces of rock brought from Wales and Scotland. Sometimes the icebergs toppled over, or split, and lost their balance, the boulders then fell from the ice on to the submerged surface below. Many of these boulders remain to this day, both in the town of Dunstable and in various places all round. Farmers have moved most of them out of the way to fields and road-side. Others have been taken to towns and villages and placed near inns for use in mounting horses in the past. One of these boulders of large size is in Back Street, Dunstable, and two others

---

παλαίος, ancient ; λιθς, stone.

in Church Street.   There is one of great size, of calcite, close to the door of Do-little Mill, Totternhoe, and one of quartzite partly buried in Stanbridge Churchyard, which was estimated to weigh a ton before it was broken and prior to its replacement in the Churchyard.   An illustration of a glaciated block of chalk-rock from near Dunstable is given in Figure 1, and a glaciated flint in Figure 1A.   The bones, tusks, and teeth of

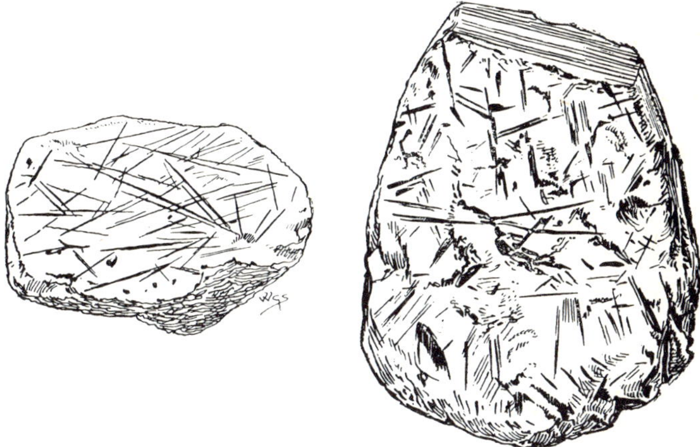

Fig. 1 and 1a.   GLACIALLY SCRATCHED CHALK ROCK AND FLINT; Dunstable, and Reach, near Leighton Buzzard.   The latter planed off and polished above by moving ice.   ½ size.

animals are less common, being more perishable.   The great Glacial Period, or period of arctic ice and partial submergence of the south of Britain under the sea, as well as the phenomena belonging to the period of the departure of extreme cold, can be well studied in South Bedfordshire. Before Primeval man appeared the land became more elevated above the sea, and Great Britain became continuous with the continent of Europe.   England, Ireland, Scotland and Northern France, as well as land extending far to the north and west towards America, were conjoined as one large country traversed by rivers, and not divided by seas.   As the land gradually rose, the ice retreated northwards and Glacial cold was at an end.

When during the Glacial Period the straits of Dover, then of great width, invaded England on one side and France on the other, and when the icy sea was full of icebergs and the temperature arctic, Primeval man and his animal companions were living in Africa, India, Central Asia, and Southern Europe. When the climate of Britain became temperate or warm and the rising surface made **Their Coming.** a wide and dry tract of land from what is now France to England then a rabble of unclothed, inarticulate savage human beings, raced over from what is now France to England. With these Primeval men came herds of tropical animals. As the land was also conjoined to northern as well as southern regions it also formed a ready trackway for animals from the north. Man himself, however, never reached to what is now Ireland and Scotland, he only overran two-thirds of southern England. Bedfordshire, and especially the neighbourhood of Dunstable, was one of the haunts of early man, and in no country can his works be better studied than near Dunstable.

The Primeval men were somewhat short in stature, with strong and curiously curved thigh bones. Their heads were long and low or flat, with receding foreheads. They had strongly projecting brows, and powerful jaws with receding chins. They possessed large back molars or wisdom teeth for chewing and breaking hard bones and nuts. These teeth have in modern races become small. The lower jaw was without the genio-hyo-glossus tubercle as in apes. These men existed in the lowest stage of savagery without articulate language and with no control of fire.

Their animal companions in Bedfordshire, as far as their bones have been at present identified, were the Bear, Hyæna, Reindeer, Mammoth, Bison, Rhinoceros, Hippopotamus, and wild Horse. Elsewhere in England bones of the Lion, wild Cat, and wild Boar have been found, with two additional species of Rhinoceros and the straight-tusked Elephant. The bones are usually found in gravel pits in company with human made flint implements of geometrical perfection of shape. The bones may be seen and studied at the British Museum

(Natural History) Cromwell Road, London, and the implements in the Pre-historic Gallery of the British Museum, Bloomsbury, the St. Albans Museum, and the Ashton Grammar School, Dunstable.

Not only is the far off Glacial Period well represented near Dunstable, but what is of greater importance is the fact that relics of Primeval man himself are comparatively abundant. Indeed the neighbourhood of Bedford is remarkable as being the first place in England where the rude flint tools of Primeval man were found, after they had been discovered and identified as of human origin in France. The first discoveries were made by Mr. James Wyatt in 1861. When the stone implements were first found it was remembered that a few similar stones were already in public museums and had remained unidentified and misunderstood for years. A remarkable instance of

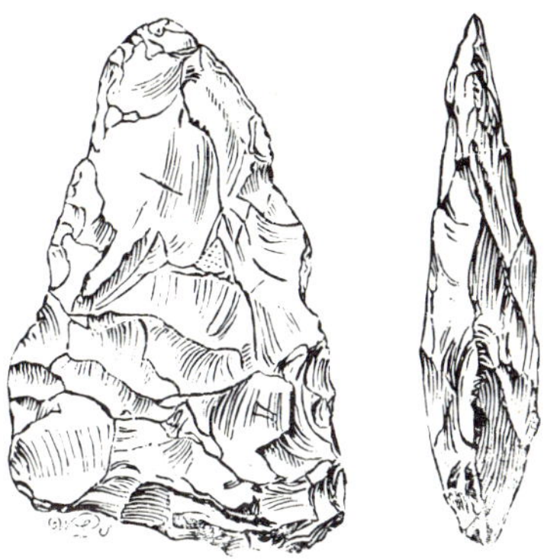

Fig. 2. A Famous Palæolithic Implement
From Dallow Farm, Luton. ½ size.
Now in the British Museum.

a much earlier and local discovery may be here mentioned. In 1890 the late Mr. John Waller, of Luton, brought the writer a number of stones for sale which he said had been collected long ago and preserved by a Mr. William Gutteridge of Dallow Farm, on the Dunstable side of Luton. Mr. Waller knew nothing of geological specimens and all the stones were quite worthless except one, which was a Palaeolithic flint implement found by

Mr. Gutteridge near his own farm in 1830. The old
piece of paper with the date was still on the stone. I
soon ascertained that the name was right, and that the
Gutteridges had held Dallow Farm for 150 years before
1830. The implement is sub-triangular in shape, bevelled
all over and rather rude, but the finder who knew nothing

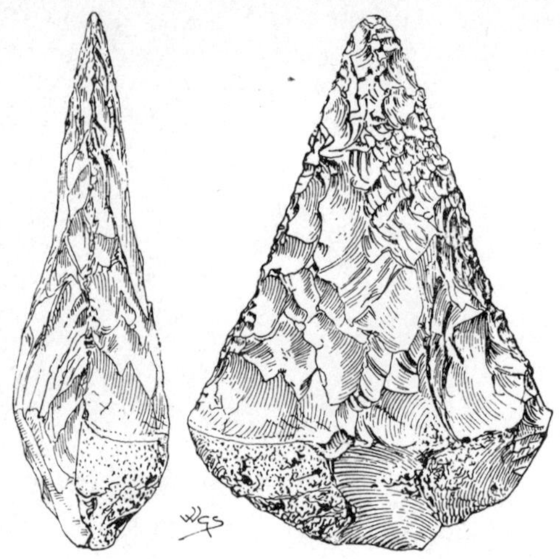

Fig. 3. POINTED PALÆOLITHIC IMPLEMENT ; Caddington. ½ size.

of flint implements, was astute enough to decide that
it was not an ordinary natural stone. A face and edge
view of the tool is illustrated in Fig. 2. The original is
now in the safe custody of the British Museum. The
most intelligent finders of Palæolithic relics amongst the
workmen of Caddington, are Mr. Coleman and his sons,
Mr. Cherry, Jun., and his son, and Messrs. Fox & Smith.

The most ancient or Palaeolithic implements are found
in gravel, or clay-pits sometimes 30 feet or more from the
surface, they range in color from dark brown to white,
and are either pointed as in Fig. 3 or ovate as in Fig. 4,
both from Caddington. In each illustration an edge and
face view is given. Both examples are now in the
British Museum.

The stratum marked Palæolithic Floor on this photograph is the old land surface at Caddington—varying in depth from 4ft. to 40ft.—on which the primeval men lived. It is strewn with their relics, visible in the photograph.

The actual living and working places of the Primeval men have been found by the writer at Caddington near Dunstable, the very places have been lighted on where the savages sat and made their weapons of stone.   The

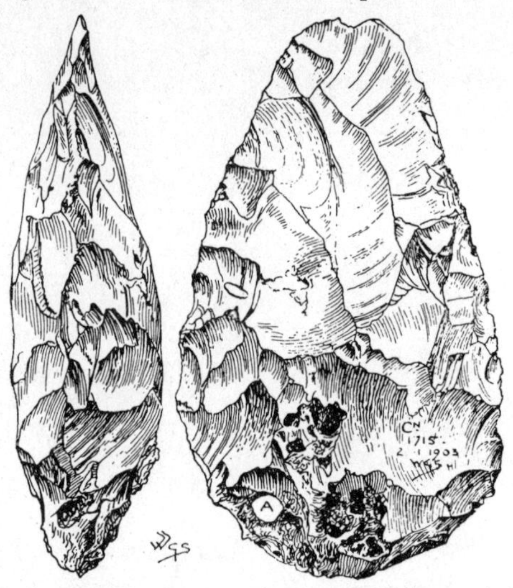

Fig. 4.   Ovate Palæolithic Implement ; Caddington.   ½ size.

discoveries have been so complete that the stone implements have been found both in a rough or initial state, and in a state of high finish.   Thousands. of flint chips have been found close to the implements, struck off in the course of flint implement manufacture.   Hundreds of these flint chips or flakes have been replaced on to each other, or on to the original implements from which they were struck tens of thousands of years ago. Examples from Caddington may be seen in the British Museum, Bloomsbury, the University Museum, Oxford, the St. Albans Museum and elsewhere.   As regards the " tens of thousands of years," Lord Avebury advocates a period of 100,000 to 240,000 in the past for the Palaeolithic period.   The lowest computation for the lowering of a valley by water, as founded on the lowering of the Thames, the Boyne, the Forth and the Tay, if applied to the lesser valley between Dunstable and Blows Downs,—the implements being found on the hill-tops,—gives 214,000 years.   Every calculation, however made, points to the same immense antiquity for Primeval man, his stone implements and his animal companions.

Primeval man appears to have been driven away southwards by a return of great, but not Arctic, cold ; by dry winters of extreme severity and succeeding abnormally stormy, wet summers.   The stormy summers loosened the frozen soil of the previous winters and buried the men and other animals amongst the stones and clay-mud where their relics are now found.   Such animals as could escape retreated southwards by land to southern Enrope, northern Africa and central Asia.   They returned decimated by famine and pestilence, to the south countries whence they came, and the country we now know as England, became entirely depopulated of human beings.

The clay-mud, stony-clay or brick-earth which submerged the Primeval men near Dunstable is named by geologists Contorted-drift.   It is the upper stiff red clay seen in some of the brick pits at Kensworth and Caddington, not esteemed for making bricks.   The finer and paler brick-earth beneath the red-clay represents the fine sediment of the muddy floods.   There is another red-clay at both villages, full of large white flints, this is of glacial origin and was there before the arrival of Primeval man, it was one of his land surfaces in which he found his flints for implement making.   The sharpest and most perfect implements are found in what, by its obviously horizonal stratification, is water-laid material. The water in Primeval human times descended from heights which do not now exist.   At that time 100,000 to 200,000 years ago, the present valleys only existed in an initial state.

After the depopulation of Britain, a vast time elapsed before the return of man.   The Southern **Prehistoric and Ancient British times.** parts had become entirely forest, bush or bog, the present valleys had been washed out.

The hills round Dunstable were covered, where the chalk now is, with low stunted bushes, where the stoney-clay is, with trees ; the valleys where

Totternhoe, Eaton Bray, Stanbridge, and Tilsworth now are were swamps. The sea had then broken once more through the Straits of Dover and the English Channel and North Sea had been formed.

As Britain was cut off from the Continent and as the barbarians of Northern Europe, perhaps the descendants of the Primeval men, were long in learning how to make boats, it was very long indeed before a new race of men arrived here.

That they did at length arrive and that they reached where Dunstable now is, is certain, as their implements and works, and probably their bones, still exist in the neighbourhood.

The newer race is known as the Neolithic* race, because **Neolithic Men.** the men were the makers of the newer sorts of stone implements, from those used by the Primeval men, different in shape, and in later times ground to a cutting upper edge. Figs. 5 and 6.

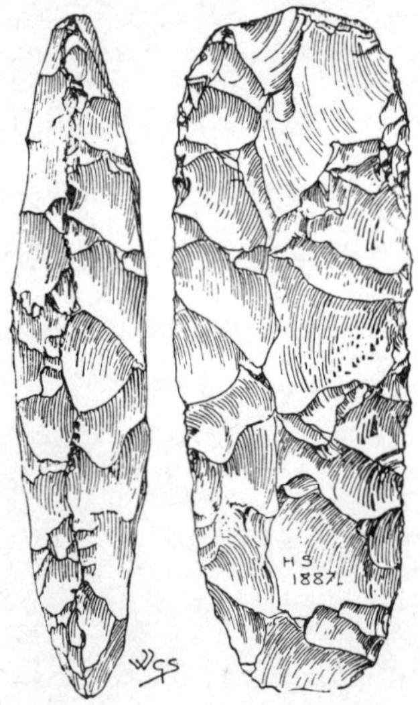

Fig. 5.   CHIPPED, UNPOLISHED CELT;
Kensworth. ½ size.

The early Neolithic men, like their predecessors, were somewhat short in stature, 5ft. 5in. in average height for the men; 4ft. 9½in. for the women, their heads were long as in their predecessors, not round as in some of their successors, their faces were oval, with brow-ridges much less developed than in the Primeval men. The Neolithic men were unacquainted with metals, but had control of fire. They stood perfectly upright and were articulate. At the time of their arrival in Britain by rafts, and in canoes hewn or burnt out of tree trunks, they were rude farmers, potters, spinners, weavers, hunters, and fishermen.

---

* νέος, new ; λίθος, stone.

They were the Silures of Tacitus, the Iberians of ancient Spain or Iberia; they erected cromlechs where stones were present and buried their dead in long, not round, tumuli. Their speech was probably involved, but of Basque or Iberian origin, not Aryan, Indian, or Sanscrit. The Basque language is still spoken in the mountainous borders of northern Spain. The Paleolithic men did not bury their dead, the Neolithic not only buried their friends, but they venerated or feared them when dead, and perhaps thought they might live again as they sometimes buried pots, ornaments, tools, weapons and even food in their graves.

When successive hordes of these men

Fig. 6. POLISHED NEOLITHIC CELT;
Dunstable. ½ size.

landed from their rafts they brought with them, for the first time, the short-horned ox, the horned sheep, the goat, the hog, and the dog. They also brought wheat, barley, peas, and millet. They cultivated apples, pears, bullace, and flax.

When Britain was depopulated, some of the larger animals, such as could withstand cold survived, amongst these were the wild boar, wild cat, wild horse, red-deer, Irish-elk, moose, reindeer, wolf, brown and grisly bear, and the gigantic ox or auroch, or, as latinized by Cæsar, urus, named by zoologists *Bos primigenius*.

Some of the newly imported animals escaped and herded with the survivals and so cross-breeds arose.

Traces of the Neolithic men are seen near Dunstable in the ruined long barrow in Union Street and a presumed long barrow on Dunstable Downs. The bones of the imported animals are all very common near Dunstable; they are frequent in the fields, but a knowledge of bones is necessary for their recognition, many thousands have been found in the pre-historic pits near Maiden Bower. The bones of some of the older animals are also found,

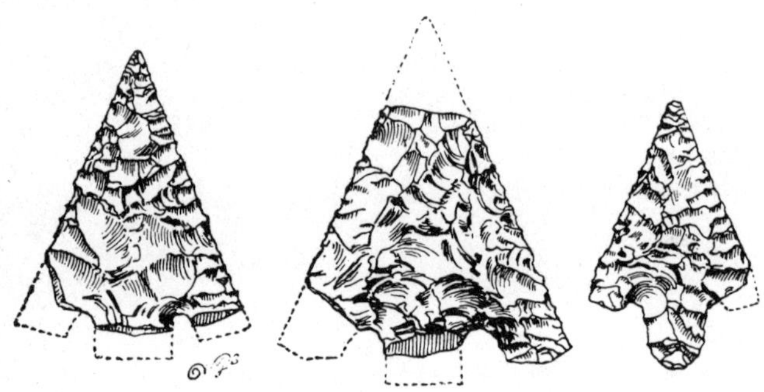

Fig. 7. ARROW-HEADS; Leagrave. Actual size.

as those of *Bos primigenius*, caught and chopped up for food by the ancient Britons, near Maiden Bower. Last and not least of the traces are—the stone axes, adzes, knives, scrapers, hammers, and spear, and arrow-heads— Fig. 7. Some of these as stone-knives and scrapers are very common, others less so.

Some of the workmen employed in the fields are expert in their knowledge of antiques and bones. The chief of these, unrivalled in local topographical knowledge and acquaintance with pottery, bones, and the different ancient implements of flint is Mr. Thomas Cumberland, farm workman of Leagrave, to whom I, and many other antiquaries are deeply indebted.

The Dunstable chalk has a remarkable power of hardening and preserving bones, so much is this the case that bones probably 10,000 or 20,000 years old are frequently disinterred in perfect condition, as white and smooth as ivory, but almost as hard as stone. It is therefore often impossible to name the age of a bone, especially if it belongs to one of the more ancient animals that survived through Paleolithic to Neolithic times. It is the same with the so-called Neolithic implements; they were made for tens of centuries without change of form, and as flint is an almost imperishable stone is it often difficult to state a probable age within a thousand years. Most of the newer or Neolithic tools date from 2,000 to 20,000 years ago. Antiquaries term such antiques "recent." The age of the tools is often indicated by the mineral condition and surroundings, as pottery, metal, bones, antlers, etc. Many Neolithic objects are similar with those of the Bronze Age which followed and isolated objects may belong to either. Long study and experience elucidates much.

For a long time unknown in periods of years, the Neolithic or Iberian people held possession of Britain. During the latter part of this time the Neolithic race of France, Spain and Germany were being invaded from the **The Bronze Age.** east by another people, named the Celtic Aryans, who differed from the short, dark, long-headed Neolithic people, in being tall and round-headed. They also differed in possessing a knowledge of bronze. The stone axe and stone knife of the Iberian was overcome by the bronze sword and bronze dagger of the invading Bronze Age folk. The Celtic Aryans or Celts were of Indo-European origin.

Like their Neolithic predecessors when the Aryan Celts had once dominated France they decided upon invading Britain. This invasion, in well-built boats, probably occupied hundreds of years. There were two groups—perhaps more—of Celtic Aryans. The first to arrive were the so-called Goidels or Gaels of Ireland, the Isle of Man, and the northern Highlands. The second group, in a higher stage of civilization, arrived centuries after, and is represented by the ancient people of Wales with parts of Cumbria and Cornwall. These were the Britons or Brythons.

The tall fair-haired Belgæ or Kymri, who came for plunder, pressed the Celtæ and occupied the country south of the Thames, they hardly reached Bedfordshire, although they entered the valley of the Lea.

The Celtic Aryans, or ancient Britons, averaged 5 feet 8½ inches in height for the males, and the women were also generally tall. Their skulls were broad or round with strongly developed brow ridges and powerful jaws. They were a light-haired people with blue eyes. They were chiefly farmers like the Neolithic folk, but in a far higher stage of civilisation; the farmers used bronze reaping hooks, the builders were able to erect Stonehenge. The men carried daggers and sometimes axes of bronze. Men and women were clothed alike in woollen or linen tunics with trousers tightened at the ankle. They wore sandals of leather. The women were decorated with necklaces of amber or gold, they wore brooches, pins, rings, buckles, and armlets of bronze or gold.

The domestic animals were the same in the Bronze Age as in the Neolithic. With improved tools and improved methods agriculture greatly advanced. Although metal was common for weapons and tools, poorer folk still used the old stone implements.

The Bronze Age people usually burned their dead, although inhumation was not entirely abolished. When burials took place the body was placed on its side in a contracted position with the knees drawn up under the chin. The body was sometimes tied up in this doubled-up position with rope before burial. These contracted interments often occur side by side with cremations in the round tumuli on Dunstable Downs. In cremations the ashes were usually collected and placed in earthen jars for burial, but sometimes, as on Dunstable Downs a small hole was dug in the chalk and the ashes were placed in the hole and covered up. The people lived in wig-wam huts built over small shallow excavations, with sticks, skins, and turf, some of the better class lived in round houses built of stakes and thatched with straw or covered with straw mats. Dunstable is particularly rich in remains of the Bronze Age people who held the country for a very long time before the Roman Conquest.

Ancient British remains are so abundant at Dunstable,
The Celtic especially on the west and north-west side
name, of what that there can be no doubt of the existence
is now of a large British population here before
Dunstable. the Roman Conquest. The place probably
had a name and the name would belong in one branch
of the ancient Celtic language. The Romans often
adopted Celtic names, but as these native names were
very harsh and gutteral the invaders could neither
pronounce nor understand them. The Romans called the
place, we now call Dunstable,—Durocobrivæ, this was
the *written* Roman name in imitation of an ancient
British *spoken* name.

The ancient name is therefore hidden in the Roman
word Durocobrivæ. Some Celtic scholars have suggested
Dwr-y-coed-bryf (pronounced Dōōr-y-koyd-briev) as the
precursor of Durocobrivæ. In modern Welsh, Dwr
means water, coed—a wood, and bryf—prey or beasts.
If this name is accepted, the name would mean the
place where water, wood and animals of the chase
abound. But there was no water on the site of
Dunstable in ancient British or Roman times.
A more probable suggestion is that the first part
of the name was not Dwr, but a derivative of Duroco,
a word equal to the Welsh dōr and drws; the Irish
dorus—a door; and the modern English word door
or portico. Dr. John Rhys, professor of Celtic to the
University of Oxford says that although the etymology
is tolerably clear the meaning is not exactly evident. He
suggests that Duroco possibly refers to the entrances
of strongholds or temples. The latter part of the word
he would refer to briv—a bridge. But objection must be
taken to both Dwr—water and briv—bridge, as neither
water or bridges were characteristic of Durocobrivæ.
The real foundation of the first syllable of the Roman
word was probably Drws. There is still a Drws-y-coed
in Carnarvonshire, meaning an entrance or door to the
wood, and a similar name might well have been the
foundation of Durocobrivæ and have referred to the
two British trackways which entered the primeval woods
on the west side of where Dunstable now stands.

Dr. Rhys, in writing to me as to the meaning of Durocobrivæ, and after considering my doubts as to the value of briv, or bridge for the terminal syllable of the name, says the name might possibly be divided as Duro-cobrivis, but what Celtic word cobrivis could have been derived from would mean he could not suggest. He says, however, that there is a Welsh word, rhiu, an incline or hillside and a compound cyf-riu is conceivable,—though not actual as far as is known to Dr. Rhys,—meaning a group of hilly inclines, Cyfriu would be in early Welsh comriv with an inevitable tendency to become cobriv. This suggestion would make the ancient name Dor-cobriv or Drws-comriv to mean the hill-side opening, or door. This derivation suits the situation of Durocobrivæ better than any other. In modern Welsh Drws is used in place-names to indicate the upper opening into a narrow valley below, as Drws-y-coed already mentioned and Drws-y-Nant, in Merionethshire. " Leighton Gap " is an old name for an opening from the Icknield Way (West Street).

Another curious fact in reference to the ancient British name must be given, Dr. Rhys in his *Celtic Britain* says that the etymology of Durocobrivis suggests the possibility of some of the *duro* names being of the same kind as *Forum Juli*, *Forum Voconi* and the like in Gaul, Spain and Italy. In this connexion it seems remarkable that in the Itinerary of Richard of Cirencester (probably a forgery, but for which the forger might have had some genuine foundation) the Durocobrivæ of Antoninus is replaced by *Forum Dianæ*. Forum Dianæ in connection with Durocobrivæ, is extensively found on modern maps of Roman Britain. The Itinerary of Richard of Cirencester was written in 1747, by Dr. Charles Julius Bertram, Professor of English at Copenhagen.

No original of Richard's supposed Itinerary is known to exist. The Roman name of Forum Dianæ for the British town which preceded Dunstable would mean the market-place of Diana, the goddess of hunting and would at first sight appear to be a purely Roman name, not founded on any British precursor. In this connexion it is again both remarkable and confusing to find that there once lived a Celtic princess, who after death was deified under the name of Diana, the latter name being founded, not on the name of the Roman Diana but on the Celtic Di-anav which means—without blemish. It must be remembered therefore that there was a British as well as a Roman Diana.

These are rude in character and made of gold, silver, tin, and copper, they are usually small, **Ancient British Coins.** concave on one side and convex on the other, the uninscribed examples are the older. Numerous examples have been found close to Dunstable, a splendid uninscribed example, in gold, and as large as a florin, was found at Leighton Buzzard in 1849. A gold coin of Tasciovanus inscribed TASCIO RICON, has been found at Dunstable, and similar examples, including one of ADDEDOMAROS, in gold have been found at Limbury. Large numbers of British coins have been found at Limbury, Sandy, and Biggleswade. Others have been recorded from Arlesey, Stondon. Baldock, Langford, Clifton, Potton, Girtford, Shefford, and Holwell. A common emblem on Ancient British coins is a rude galloping horse, or a rude face, badly imitated from a Greek or Roman example which had come into the hands of the later British coiners; the Macedonian Philippus was one of the originals of the British copies, this was brought from Greece through Gaul to Britain.

CHAPTER III.

The Famous Prehistoric Remains close to Dunstable.

THIS Bronze Age camp is easily found at 1½ miles from the middle of Dunstable to the west. The methods of reaching the place by green-way and field - paths are described in Chapter XI. The green-way is the more pleasant, the field-way more direct. The late Mr. James Wyatt, of Bedford, suggested that, as Maiden Bower is a Celtic camp, an original Celtic name of Magh-dun-bárr lies embedded in the modern appellation, "Magh" being the plain on which the camp stands, "dun," or "din," being the hill-fortress—for the camp is situated on very high ground—and "bárr" being the top. In other words, Magh-dun-bárr means the camp, or fortress, on the flat hill-top. The pronunciation, only easy to a Welshman, is Mach-dinbár. The name occurs several times in the thirteenth century *Dunstable Chronicle* as Maydenbure, Maydenburi, and Maydenaburi. The term "bower" is a mere modern corruption, unworthy of notice. I have heard the older folk term the camp the "castle" and the "cassie"; both words are synonymous with camp or fortress.

Maiden Bower (Fig. 8) measures within its banks 775 feet from north to south, and 750 feet from east to west. It encloses 10 acres 2 rods and 25½ square yards; the width of the vallum or enclosing earthen bank, varies from 16 to 28 feet, and the height of the vallum from 4 ft. 6 in. to 10 ft. 6 in. Originally, there was a dyke or

ditch all round from 18 to 20 feet wide, and as deep as
the banks were high; in some places the width of the
ditch can be traced to 32 feet.   The former owner once
told me that when carts were taken out of the chief
entrance—the one towards Dunstable, from which an
old trackway to Dunstable can sometimes be seen—

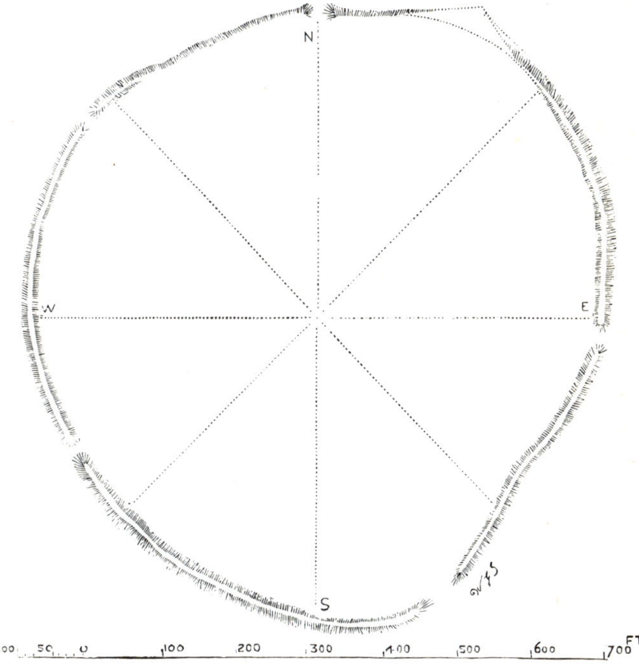

Fig. 8.

a hollow sound could be heard as if the carts were
passing over a hollow chamber.   No excavations
have been made at any time, but lime-burners have
nearly reached the western edge in their excavations
for chalk.   The five original entrances still remain.   They
are not cartways made by farmers.   During recent excavations an old trackway from the north was found, and

on it an iron tanged arrow or spear head with a socket for the insertion of a shaft. The road led towards Sewell, where there are abundant springs and plenty of water. The camp itself is 160 feet above the springs and entirely without water. On the north side of the camp, and on the north side of the railway, a Dene Hole was cut into in 1860; it can be partly seen near the level of the rails now. It was exposed to 116 feet, and the usual holes were observed in the sides for the insertion of horizontal planks of wood by which the hole could be descended as by a ladder. It had been filled in with chalk refuse, flints, pieces of broken British pottery, a Roman tile, and burnt wood. This Dene Hole is marked " Well " on the 6-inch Ordnance map, in characters which indicate a Roman well. Quite lately the North-Western Railway Company, who were badly wanting water, imagined the map to be right, and set a number of men to work to farther dig out this supposititious " well." It is not necessary to state the result. The Celts did not dig wells 160 feet deep when abundant water was only a few feet off in the valley just below.

During the process of chalk-digging, in 1897-99, at 50 to 87 feet from the western bank, five ancient excavations were dug into; the northernmost was 8 feet across and 10 feet deep, filled in with chalk rubble; the next was 4 feet square with rounded corners and 4 ft. 6 in. deep; it contained broken-up human bones, and was a re-interment. The two next were 20 feet and 40 feet long and 10 feet wide; they were full of broken bones of the Celtic ox and other Bronze-Age animals, all broken for the marrow they once contained, and mixed with chalk rubble, rude British pottery, flint flakes, and a flint polishing-stone, as used in ancient British times for polishing flint-axes.

The fifth excavation, to the south, was a very large one, but only 4 feet deep; it was filled, like the last, with bones, flints and rubble. A later grave had been dug through the middle of this filled-in hole to two feet below the original bottom. At the base of the grave lay a perfect human skeleton extended on its back with the head to the east. The head was 51 feet from the bank, the teeth were considerably split and broken, as if the original owner had, before death, received a severe blow on the mouth, and the left thigh-bone exhibited a cut in the middle of the shaft as if from a slash from a sword. The skeleton appeared to be only 300 or 400 years old, and was kept by Messrs. Forder and Co., the owners of the lime works.

At Totternhoe.

Totternhoe Knoll in the distance.

The Totternhoe Camps and Knoll are a little more than a mile to the west of Maiden Bower, **Totternhoe Knoll.** and can easily be reached by the Greenways mentioned under *Pleasant Walks*. The eastern side of the camp will be reached first with the wide, straight ditch more than 200 feet long. This, and the plateau beyond, and the ditch to the north, seems to be Roman work ; the elevated bank at the north-east angle is characteristically Roman. On the south is a natural precipice. The plateau is about 500 feet long, and bounded on the west by a British ditch, or a British ditch altered in Roman times. A small Roman

D

camp seems to have been constructed close to a Bronze-Age look-out station.   We can enter the British camp by crossing the ditch and mounting the vallum or earthern bank, or by one of the two entrances at the north and south angles.   We are then in a large circular enclosure, with the great knoll or fire-beacon in the centre ; further to the west is another irregularly circular enclosure of smaller size.   On the north-east side is a wide and deep depression like the mouth of a well, locally called the Money-pit (see *Folk-Lore*).   It is sometimes called a well.   This depression probably represents the entrance to a subterranean store-chamber of Bronze-Age times. Nothing but careful excavation can finally explain its purpose.   It would probably repay exploration.

Scattered round the great Fire-knoll, except on the southern side, are more than thirty shallow saucer-like depressions, each about 8 feet in diameter, but varying larger and smaller ; these are probably the sites of huts of Bronze-Age date—the huts of the men who were stationed on the hill to keep watch over the plains beneath and over the heights of Dunstable Downs, Ivinghoe, and Edlesborough Hill.   The undulated ground in the valley on the western side of the camp is modern work.

Wanlud's Bank.   This Bronze-Age sub-circular camp is close to Leagrave Station on the Midland Railway, with the source of the river Lea on its north-western side.   It is a little more than three miles north-east of Dunstable, and of the same age and date as Maiden Bower.   There is a public foot-path past the camp on the east side of the river.   This camp, although of Celtic origin, was doubtlessly used, as were many other British camps in later years, by the Romans and Anglo-Saxons.   As in Maiden Bower, the present name is a modern corruption of an older one, perhaps founded on the Anglo-Saxon " Wealhas " —Welshmen, or foreigners—the camp of the defeated opponents.   Like Maiden Bower, Wanlud's Bank and its neighbourhood has in the past yielded large numbers of stone axes, arrow-heads and scrapers.

The destroyed circular camp formerly near Leighton Buzzard was situated on the Heath. It resembled Maiden Bower, but in the enclosures of 1798 was completely levelled with the ground, and not a trace now remains except the ancient name of the field in which it once stood, viz., " Craddock's "—probably founded on the Celtic Caradog. The camp was situated on the north-west of Sandy Lane, 1½ miles north of Leighton Buzzard, in the fields south-west of Heath and Reach ; its nearest banks were a quarter of a mile west of the large pond, on the west side of Heath and Reach Road. On the south side of Sandy Lane, in the Plantation, are two very large mounds, marked " Tumuli " on the 6-inch Ordnance Map.

The five Knolls on the brow of Dunstable Downs, overlooking the valley and visible for many miles from the lower grounds, are Bronze Age erections set up to commemorate certain notable dead of that **The Five Knolls Tumuli.** period. They have been opened in times past, but no satisfactory reports, according to modern views, have been published. They probably contained contracted interments with pottery and flint implements, possibly also the ashes belonging to cremations. I have part of a human skull and some broken pelvic bones scratched out of these mounds by rabbits.

The depressions close to the tumuli are the places whence the materials were dug for the erection of the mounds, other depressions are hut-remains. There are also Bronze Age trackways, one leads from a circular hut foundation near the seat on the hill facing the Rifle Volunteer inn. In favourable seasons the track of this path may be seen to descend the hill and cross the fields to the western end of the Green Way plantation, and enter Maiden Bower by the main opening.

There were formerly two other tumuli, on the other side of the road, to the south. These were levelled and rifled long ago, but on a re-excavation made in 1887, by permission of the owner of the land, Mr. F. T. Fossey, I disinterred a crouching boy from the southern tumulus and a crouching woman and child from the northern platen. The woman was surrounded with

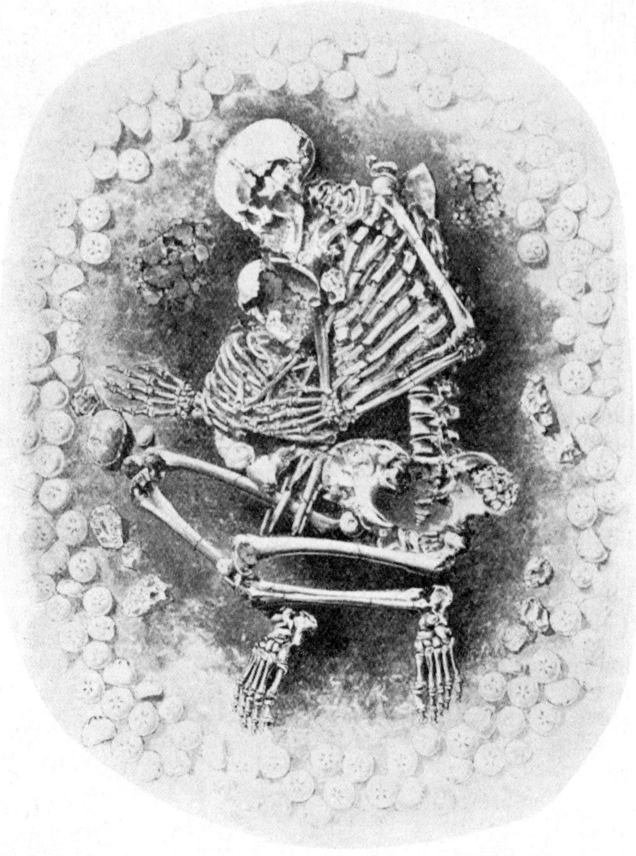

                                                    [*Drawn by the Author.*

Woman and Child of the Bronze Age.
Disinterred from a tumulus on Dunstable Downs by the Author in 1887.

fossil *Echini*, broken British pottery, and indifferent flint implements. There had been in each case a central interment, with others round the circumference. Both the skeletons came from the circumference.

British hut remains are numerous in the neighbourhood of Dunstable. There is a fine collection on Blows Downs on the west side of the lime works, others are on the brow **British Hut Remains.** of these Downs overlooking Southern Dunstable. There are several close to the Five Knolls on Dunstable Downs and others looking southwards over Pascombe Pit. There is a fine group on the east of Valence End Farm, on the slope of the Downs on the road from the Plough inn, Edlesborough, to Whipsnade.

Whilst digging for chalk at the Limeworks on Blows Downs in 1888, eight British Huts were destroyed, they averaged, when cut into, about twelve feet in diameter and three feet in depth. On the floor of one of these a human skeleton was found spread out at full length, it represented a man who when alive was 5ft. 10ins. high. There was a piece of an ancient British pot, a block of iron pyrites and several artificially struck flint flakes on the floor with the bones. I was only able to secure part of this skeleton, as the workmen, although previously instructed by me, wheeled most of the bones, including the skull, with chalk, into the kilns for lime.

Isolated hut remains occur in all directions on the hills, some occur on Warden Hill and Gully Hill, Luton, others on Ivinghoe and Edlesborough Hills. When they occur on hill sides, a channel for drainage may often be seen towards the slope of the hill as in some of the examples overlooking Pascombe Pit.

CHAPTER IV.

Dunstable in Roman Times.

IN the Itinerary of Antoninus, a Roman work written in the beginning of the third century (not by either of the Antonines, but by Antoninus Caracallus), an ancient British position, which gave place to a Roman station, is given under the name of Durocobrivæ. This Durocobrivæ is stated to have been twelve Roman miles from Verulámium (St. Albans), and sixteen or seventeen from Magiovinium (Fenny Stratford). A Roman mile contained 1,613 yards, or 147 yards less than a British mile. Judging by the distances given by Antoninus and the numerous Roman remains that have been found in and close to Dunstable, there can be no doubt that the Roman station was on the west side of the town. The village now called Totternhoe, judging from the large number of Roman relics found in and close to that village, was in immediate contact with the station itself. Maiden Bower, Sewell, and Totternhoe Hill were strongly held by the Romans. The total absence of water, except pools from land drainage, not always present, on the east side of Dunstable would prevent any British village or Roman station being fixed there. No Roman remains have at present been found in that direction. The ancient Britons, as well as the Romans, must have chiefly depended upon the water of Well Head, of Totternhoe, and Sewell, for their existence, and it is round these positions, and between these places and High Street Dunstable, that the Roman remains are found.

Ther: is no meaning to the Roman name Duroco-brivæ; it is a Latinized phonetic rendering

Meaning of the Roman name. of the ancient British name, Dorcobriv.

Modern authors have done their best to obscure the meaning and position of Durocobrivæ. It has been suggested that the Itinerary of Antoninus might possibly be wrong as regards this district; and that Durocobrivæ and Magiovinium had been accidentally transposed. On some modern maps this transposition has actually been effected. In some recent books both names have been made to do duty for Dunstable, and in some cases " Forum Dianæ " has been engraved over Maiden Bower, on the suggestion of Thomas Reynolds in his *Iter Britanniarum*. Wherever the name of Street occurs as an ancient name it suggests Roman occupation or a Roman road. It is derived from the Latin *stratum*, and occurs close to Dunstable, in Watling Street, Markyate Street, and Street Fields. Near by there are later forms of "street" in Stony and Fenny-Stratford and Streatley.

Roman names appear to survive in the district, as Campum Downum and Comp, near Totternhoe, and in the local personal name of Costin, which seems synonymous with the " master Constantine "—" magistri Constantini " of the " *Annales Dunstaplia*," under A.D. 1273. The name of Bacchus appears in old Kensworth leases.

Dunstable is crossed in the Market Place by two ancient roads called Watling Street and the Icknield Way. The Icknield Way was ancient British before it was Roman. The British Road or Icknield Way

The Ancient Roads. (Church Street and West Street) occupies the original site as used in ancient British times. It is not so with the precursor of the Roman Road named Watling Street. The ancient British precursor still exists near the West end of West Street in the " Green Way " or " Drovers' Way," to Totternhoe Hill. It leaves Maiden Bower a little to the right and Totternhoe Knoll a little to the left.

Before Roman times then, the crossing was near the west end of West Street and not in the middle of the town as now, where marked by a cross on the map.

The Roman engineers, when they arrived from London to where Markyate Street now is, were using the ancient British road, but when they reached Markyate Street they found this road to be carried over very unsuitable ground for Roman purposes. The British road ran partly on the side of a long hill, past the north side of where Kensworth Church and Down's Farm now are, to the Green Lane, near the end of West Street. The Romans kept to the bottom of the valley, and made a new piece of road from where Markyate Street now is, to Hockliffe, leaving the sites of Kensworth Church and Down's Farm more than three-quarters of a mile to the west.

There are then three important ancient roads in and close to Dunstable. The Watling Street or great military road of the Romans passing through the town from south to north. The inferior ancient British precursor of this road near the end of West Street, and the Icknield way passing through Dunstable from east to west. There are minor roads of great antiquity, bearing traditional names. All are marked on the accompanying map.

The Watling Street (the Via Vitellina of antiquaries) starts from the south-east coast, from **The Course of the Roman Roads.** Richboro', Dover, and Lymne. Roads from these three places meet at Canterbury, and the road passes on to Rochester, South Fleet, and London. At London it joins roads from Pevensey and Chichester. Watling Street next passes through Barnet to St. Albans, Dunstable and Fenny Stratford, Towcester, Daventry, Stafford, Chesterton, and Chester, and lastly the road is continued to Holyhead.

The Roman road itself is sometimes laid bare in, or near Dunstable. Near Kensworth Lynch it occurs at from two to four feet beneath the present high road. A few years ago I saw 165 feet of the old road exposed in a cleared-out ditch, between the " Horse and Jockey " and " Packhorse " inns, the width exposed was some four or five feet. The old road was two feet beneath the present road, perfectly flat and even, and so hard and compact that it could only be pierced with difficulty. The surface

From a Drawing] **Market Day, Dunstable.**—Early Morning. [by the Author.

was made up of closely compacted flints of various sizes,
pieces of hard sandstone and other stones such as are found
on the surface on Kensworth Common and Caddington
Hill. Nothing of special note was thrown out with the
excavated material. At my request a hole was picked
through the surface of the old road and the compact
stratum of stones was found to be about nine inches deep.

During the drainage works in 1901 the Roman road
was exposed in front of the Town Hall, Dunstable, at a
depth of 8 feet.

The meaning of the word Watling, in Watling Street,
has often been discussed, it is probably a modern form
of the Anglo-Saxon Wætlinga Stræte, and this a form of
a possible Roman Via Vitellina. What Vitellina may
mean is uncertain, but the Celtic name which must have
preceded it, and on which it was founded must have
commenced with Gw, and may therefore have been
derived from Gwyddel. Vitellina is possibly a Roman
form of this. The road went direct to the country of
the so-called Gwyddels or Goidels in North Wales,
where their numerous hut remains are still called Cyttiau
Gwydellod, meaning the huts or styes of foreigners, or
Gwyddels, Goidels, or Gaels,—not Celts.

The Icknield Way starts from Caister in Norfolk,
where it receives branches from the north-
The Icknield east coast, viz., from Brancaster, Cromer,
Way. Burgh Castle, and Dunwich. From Caister
it passes through Icklingham to Bury St. Edmunds, and
so to Royston and Dunstable. From Dunstable it
passes to Wallingford, where it crosses the Thames.
From Wallingford it goes on to Speen, Old Sarum, and
Dorchester. After the Thames is crossed the road is
named West Ridge : north of Dorchester it is Adling
Street, and south the Ridgeway. There is a Maiden
Bower near Dunstable and a Maiden Castle near
Dorchester.

This is the Via Icenorum, Via Iceniana, and Icenine
Way of antiquaries, the road to the country of that
section of the ancient Britons named the Iceni by
Tacitus, a country now represented by Norfolk, Suffolk,
Cambridgeshire, and Huntingdonshire. On ancient

British coins the name occurs as ECEN; this would indicate the name of the people to be the Eceni.

Fifty years ago there existed a large circular and perfectly flat earthen platform at the foot of the Combe. It was apparently of Roman work and 87 feet in Diameter. Immediately above it, on the hill-top, is the traditional site of the first Dunstable Church, probably a Roman shrine. The platform had every appearance of being a suitable place for Roman games, such as wrestling, boxing, and sword-fighting; it was quite large enough for a display of horsemanship. The spectators would all be seated on higher ground, as if in a natural horse-shoe amphitheatre.

Roman Platform, at base of Pascombe Pit.

When the Rifle Volunteer movement was started at Dunstable, in 1859, this platform was used for the erection of targets and markers' huts, and greatly injured. When a new series of step-like platforms, and a long, deep hole, were made, in 1902, for new targets, the place was to such an extent destroyed that at the present time only faint traces of the original work can be seen. A long transverse excavation was made right through the artificial work into the undisturbed chalk below. The excavations showed that numerous large wooden piles had been fixed in the chalk, apparently with the view of keeping the chalk rubble in position. The excavated material of 1902 consisted wholly of chalk from the valley; no flints from the clay above occurred. Amongst the rubble were numerous artificially struck flint-flakes, a globular British corn-muller, and a flint scraper. It therefore seems clear that the material used for raising the platform was of British date, dug from the valley and thrown up after British times when minor flint tools were disregarded.

Pieces of Roman pottery, large and small, chiefly of cinerary urns are to be found all over the Dunstable district; they occur in the fields, on the hills, in the valleys and frequently in the town gardens. Vases are seldom found in a perfect state as the material of which they are made is fragile,

Roman Pottery.

and if perfect when found in the earth they are usually broken in exhumation. A few smaller examples have been found entire.

Fig. 9.   ROMAN VASES, ¼ actual size, Dagnall.

A considerable number of cinerary urns found entire, but broken by the workmen in extraction, have been found near Dagnall. A large number, but all broken, have been found in Roman waste pits in West Field, Totternhoe. A small entire example at the foot of Totternhoe Hill. A large number have been met with in waste pits on Kensworth Common, others close by, some entire with burnt human bones. Pieces of Roman pots have been thrown out from graves in Kensworth churchyard. Entire urns with human bones have been found in the fields behind the Markyate Street Cell. A large number, some at first entire in the brick fields, south of Caddington. Many at Leagrave.

At Kensworth Common pieces of large amphoræ have been found together with pieces of large earthern pans, some of which when entire would have been large enough for brine pans for salting meat.

Many pieces of Castor ware have been found, some pieces with traces of paint, others covered with a vitreous glaze or ornamented with engine turned patterns. Pieces of mortaria are common. Examples of broken red ware termed Samian, some with egg and tongue ornament are frequent as are pieces of local imitation red ware. Some examples of red ware bear the name of the potter as,—Nicephor. f. Cinetvm. Conativs. f., &c. The initial f. stands for *fecit* or " made it," as " Nicephorus made it." Sometimes the initial m. occurs, this stands for *manu*, " by the hand of " or of, which means *officina*, " from the worshop of."

Various Roman Antiquities found near Dunstable.

A curb of nine large links in brass on the Downs, near Dagnall, in 1855.

A small fibula of bronze found by Mr. F. T. Fossey in a field on the east side of Whipsnade turning near the beech-trees on Dunstable Downs, 1896.

Two small bronze rings, Dunstable Downs, same site as last, 1897.

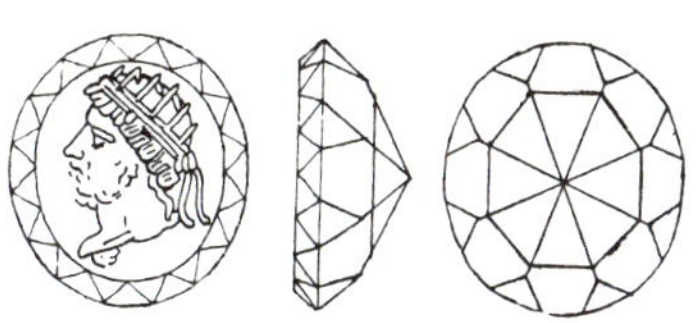

Fig. 10.   Roman Intaglio Gem, Maiden Bower,
actual size.

An intaglio in translucent paste, with head of Carausias, a.d. 287-293. Maiden Bower, 1900. Fig. 10.

A winged phallus of bronze, with ring for suspension, used as a charm against the " evil eye " and for the promotion of fertility. Totternhoe. Given to me by Mr. F. Cartwright, solicitor, Dunstable.

Small pieces of Roman glass. Totternhoe, Maiden Bower, Caddington. A flat spindle-whorl made of burnt clay. Kensworth Common.

A number of broken inscribed stones are locally said to have been once found in " 14-acres field," one quarter of a mile north of Kensworth Church and close to the ancient British road. They were taken to the house of the Rev. Henry Windsor, at that time vicar, who preserved them till his death, after which they disappeared.

Roman querns (hand-mills), of Hertfordshire con-glomerate and Andernach volcanic basalt, often broken, are by no means uncommon in fields, ditches, and gardens. Mr. John Batchelor has several perfect examples found at Dagnall. I have a perfect specimen from Leagrave, where it had been found and placed under a water-butt to prevent the bottom from rotting. I have a roughed out unfinished example from Blows Down, and a large number of pieces.

Whilst the Dunstable drainage works were being executed, in 1901, two Roman refuse-pits were cut into; one of these was in Cross Street, which the pit crossed near the middle at right angles; the other was in Chapel Alley. The Roman surface was here only about 1 ft. 3 ins. below the present surface. The pits were four feet across, and the bottom of each about 6 ft. 9 ins. below the present surface. They were full of Roman pottery and bones. The pottery included the so-called Samian, imported from France and Italy in Roman times, imitation local Samian, black Castor ware, ware with engine-turned patterns, some with a vitreous glaze, and other examples of local origin. A large number of oyster-shells of Roman age were found with the pots and bones. The enterprise and energy of the ancient Romans is well shown in this trifling fact of fresh oysters being obtainable in abundance in the Roman market at Dunstable, at and probably before the time of Christ.

The discoveries of Roman waste-pits and pottery at Dunstable fall into insignificance when compared with the waste-pits found in West Field, Totternhoe, in 1899. The long trenches were not fewer than eight in number, and from 25 feet to 30 feet apart; they were full of broken Roman pottery and bones. The pottery included not only broken vases of all sorts, but floor and roof tiles and pieces of the so called Samian ware.

Other Roman waste-pits have been found in large numbers on Kensworth Common, and near Buncer's Farm, Caddington.

In the Philosophical Transactions, vol. xlv. No. 486, 1748, published 1750, there is a brief account, illustrated by a copper plate, of the discovery of a Roman tessera or

tablet of brass, dug up in Bedfordshire, near Markyate
Street, four miles to the south of Dunstable.
Roman Tessera. The description is by Mr. John Ward, F.R.S.,
but the tablet was brought to the Society by
a Mr. Samuel Clark.

The inscription is continued on the tablet from one
side to the other, and, as shown by the accompanying
illustration—one half the actual size—is very clear.

Fig. 11.   Roman Tessera, showing both sides, one-half actual size,
Markyate Street.

Tes. Dei. Mar. Sediarvm.
When the missing letters are supplied, the inscription
would probably read,—

Tessera. Dei. Martis. Sediarvm.

Tablet of the god Mars of Sediæ.

As will be seen from the illustration the tablet is
furnished with a ring for suspension. Fig. 11.

A sacred tessera like the Markyate example, in the
hands of a proper officer, authorized him to collect
contributions for sacrifices for harvest festivals and for
religious purposes generally, the tessera was suspended
by a chain, ready for production. The sacrifices and
festivals were supported by the inhabitants in the
neighbourhood of the temple, and it is probable that the
temple to Mars stood not far from where Markyate Street
now is. Although the Roman place-name Sediæ has
not been identified, it is obviously of the same class as
Durocobrivæ, the name of Roman Dunstable. The god
Mars was the tutelar deity of the place. A dedication to
Mars has been found at Barkway, not far from Royston,
Herts, and is described in the Philosophical Transactions
for 1756. The inscription begins Marti Joviali, a
complimentary epithet to Mars.

There were many kinds of Roman tesseræ, some mere tablets of wood, admitting the bearer to gladiatorial combats or games, others entitling the bearer to portions of corn, or parts of the burnt flesh of sacrifices, or for use as tablets of introduction.

ROMAN COINS FOUND AT AND NEAR DUNSTABLE.

Large numbers of coins have been found in bronze, silver, and gold. Many of the bronze examples are corroded beyond recognition. No perfect list has been kept or ever been made out.

The following are a few of the coins of some of the Roman Emperors, which have come under my notice, printed according to dates. I have many of which I am uncertain. Of others which I have named for callers, I have kept no record.

B.C. 27—AD. 14.	Augustus.	A.D. 161-169.	Faustina.
A.D. 14-37.	Tiberius.	,, 180-192.	Commodus.
,, 37-41.	Caligula.	,, 222-235.	Marcus Aurelius.
,, 41-54.	Claudius.	,, 267-273.	Tetricus.
,, 68-69.	Sergius Galba.	,, 276-282.	Probus.
,, 69.	Otho.	,, 284-313	Diocletian.
,, 69-79.	Vespasian.	,, 287-293.	Cerausius.
,, 81-96.	Domitian.	,, 293-296.	Allectus.
,, 98-117.	Tragan.	,, 305-311.	Maximianus.
,, 117-138.	Hadrian.	,, 306-337.	Constántinus.
,, 138-161.	Antoninus Pius.	,, 337.	Dalmatius.

No Roman coins were minted in Britain before the time of Diocletian.

Many Denarii of the Roman republic have also been found.

The latest Roman coin dates from A.D. 337. The **Romano-British Times.** Romans left Britain in A.D. 401-410, and between the latter date and the landing of the Jutes, in A.D. 449, the Celts were left much to themselves; at any rate, the Roman rule had passed away. The Picts, from the North, and the Saxon pirates, from the South, did not reach Dunstable.

Many traces of the post-Roman Celts have been met with near Dunstable; they are known to be post-Roman by the mingling together of Celtic and British objects. A Romano-British land-surface was cut into at Buncer's

Farm, Caddington, in 1895, and at one place there was a heap of artificially struck flint chips and flint tools, with a stone axe or two and an arrow-head. They represented a Romano-Briton's possessions. Amongst the things were two bronze Roman coins, a small piece of a Roman millstone, and several pieces of Roman pots. There were also two or three bones, the probable remains of the owner's last dinner.

In 1895 the Rev. S. A. Woolward made some excavations in the "Spinny," near West Field, Totternhoe, and he uncovered a Romano-British hut. On the hearth was a large broken-up Roman quern, of Andernach basalt, a flint scraper, knife and hone, a Roman tile, and flint flakes. The Roman things had evidently been collected together and taken home by the Briton after the departure of the Romans. One object was very curious—a piece of a Roman tile with a clear impression of the foot of a large dog; it must have been taken home as a curiosity. In the same spinny, and a short distance only from the hut, Mr. Woolward disinterred two human skulls in a fragmentary state.

The north-east corner of West Street, where the whiting sheds are, is named Cold Harbour **Cold Harbour.** on the old inch Ordnance map. The name is synonymous with Cold Shelter, and means that at some far-off time there was a building of some kind where wayfarers might find refuge, but no food. Some antiquaries believe that the name Cold Harbour invariably marks the site of a former Roman building, and that the mere name without Roman remains, is sufficient evidence of a former structure which offered a cold lodging for travellers in wild places where no better accommodation could be secured. Many antiquities, some of metal, are reported to have been found at this corner when the fir and beech plantation opposite was planted, some sixty or seventy years ago.

There is another Cold Harbour three miles south, near Dagnall. Close by a large number of Roman cinerary urns and bowls have been found. It is believed that the old shelters have only been cleared away at a comparatively late period.

E

CHAPTER V.

In Saxon and Danish Times.

SOON after the departure of the Romans the site of Dunstable was invaded by the Saxons. The date is definitely fixed by the Anglo-Saxon Chronicle in the entry for A.D. 571, which says, "This year Cuthulf fought against the Britons at Bedcanford, and took four towns, Lygean-birg and Ægeles-birg and Bænesington and Egonesham." No doubt has ever been expressed as to the identity of Bedcanford with Bedford, but different views have been published as to the three latter. The raid, as I believe, was probably made on the site of the old Bedford Road from Bedford to what is now Leagrave, and from Leagrave along the Icknield Way to Ægelesbirg, the present Edlesborough. Lyg, in Lygean-birg, was probably the British or Celtic name of the Lea, it is equivalent with Lug or slow-moving, the Saxon would make it Lyg-ea or Lyg-ean, meaning Lyg-water, and the birg was the fort or British camp on the spot, now named Wanlud's Bank. The British name of the Lea, as Lyg, is preserved in Offa's charter to the Abbot of St. Albans (A.D. 795), where Luton is called Lygetune, equivalent to Lyg or Lugtown. The Lea is twice called the Ligean in the Anglo-Saxon Chronicle under A.D. 913. Domesday changes the *y* to *i* and gives Litone for Luton. The *g* of Lugton has dropped out in the modern name of Luton. The present name of the river Lea has come about by the dropping of *y* and *g* in Lygea, and has nothing whatever to do with lea as meaning meadow land.

To reach Edlesborough from Leagrave the merciless Saxons would have to pass through, where Dunstable now stands, the wood-built Durocobrivæ of the peaceful, agricultural Romano-British. No doubt but every house was burnt and the inhabitants, young and old, butchered.

The Saxon murderers were slaughtered in similar fashion by the Danes a little later on.

From Ægelesbirg (Edlesborough) the Saxons went on to Bænesington, the present Bossington, now a positively empty name on maps—a *ton*, or town, with no houses, except a solitary modern farm-house, " Bossington " is close to Leighton Buzzard on the west, and was on the direct way to the great British camp at Craddock's by Heath. The next move was to Egonesham, probably the present Egginton, and so by Hockliffe and Battlesden, the former with earthworks and the latter a place with a notable name, and till lately with a huge monolith boulder. From Battlesden the raiders probably went on to Toddington, a place remarkable for its Saxon relics, and so once more to the Saxon main position on the Bedford Road between Barton and Silsoe.

One proof that the whole Dunstable district fell into the complete possession of the Saxons is shown by the Saxon place-names which cover the local map in every direction. Here you have the Saxon towns, houses, hills, valleys, homes, brooks, and forts. The human beings and the Celtic and Roman languages, together with the old religions and the newer Christian religion of the Romano-Britons were swept away, and replaced by things and names wholly Saxon.

It may be well to briefly review some of these local Anglo-Saxon place-names. The suffix *ton* **Saxon Place-Names.** is a good example. In Saxon times it meant a place enclosed by a fence or hedge ; the fence, in turn, usually enclosed a Saxon house of wood. This enclosure, with a single house, soon became a small village, and, in some instances, in course of years a town. Near Dunstable we have Eaton, Houghton, Milton, Slapton, Luton, Hexton, Chalton, Flitton, Marston, Weston, and Leighton. The prefix in these names either indicates some peculiarity of the place or the owner's name, as Ea-ton, Water-town, Mill-ton, Mill-town or Middle-town, and Chal-ton (farmers' town). The suffix *-ham* belongs to the same class of words; it means "home." Near Dunstable we have Studham; sometimes it is a prefix, as in Hampstead (homestead), or a middle syllable, as in Berkhampsted, Hemel-hempstead, Wheathampstead. *Stead* is equivalent with "station," therefore Hampstead is "home-station," or fixed home. The prefix indicates a local peculiarity or owner's name, as in ton. *Hoe* and *Hoo* indicate a hill, as Totternhoe, Risinghoe, Cogenhoe, Sharpenhoe, Humbershoe, and Luton Hoo. In the latter case, if Hoo is a personal name it is equivalent with Hill, and means Hoo's or Hill's Luton, just as Houghton Regis is King's Houghton. Sometimes the *h* is dropped, as in Silsoe. A ridge of a hill is indicated in Ashridge, Putteridge, and Ridgemount. Single houses are indicated by "*cot*," as Biscot (Bishop's-cot) and Hulcot. The large house, palace, or hall, is indicated by the suffix *al* or *all*, in such names as Hudnall, Dagnall, Pepsal, Kingsall, and Bibsall. A manor or piece of property is a *worth* as Kensworth, Tebworth, and Tilsworth. A ditch or entrenchment is a *grave*, as Chalgrave, Wingrave, and Leagrave. *Bury*, *burgh*, and *borough* mean a fort, a stronghold, a fortified town, village, or house, as Kingsbury, at Dunstable, and the numerous Bury-farms and Bury-fields in the district. We have also Putteridgebury, Aldbury, Soulbury, and Edlesborough. Springs and brooks are indicated by *well*, as Wellhead, Sewell, Woburn, Redbourne, Boxmoor, and Mentmore. Dry places, surrounded by swamps, are *Ayotts*. The syllable *ing* is common in place-names near Dunstable; it means a son, a descendant or member of a clan, as Egg-ing-ton, the village of the sons of the Saxon Egga. There is also Caddington, Billington, Toddington, Cheddington, Wiggington, Cublington, and Norrington. Instead of the *ton*, or village, sometimes we have the *ham*, or home, as in Bramingham. A wooded valley is a *den*, as in Gaddesden, Nettleden, Battlesden, Harpenden, and Harrowden. The fords across streams are frequent, as in Watford, Fenny

Photograph]   **High Street South, Dunstable.**   [*H. A. Strange.*

Stratford, and Bedford.   The termination *ley* means a place, as Offley, or Offa's place; Stopsley, Stewkley, Bletchley, Crawley, Olney.   The termination of culti-vated land is the *end*, as Slip-end, Charl-end, and Pepsal-end.

The Saxon names are valuable as they indicate undoubted Saxon positions. Saxon antiques and bones of the Saxon people are chiefly found in their burial places as at Dead-man's Slade, near Leighton Buzzard, Dead-man's hedge, near Leagrave, and Deadmansey near Studham.   Saxon architectural work is spread all over the district; there is work at Stevington Church, a Saxon arch at Wheathampstead Church, and Saxon work in the tower of Clapham Church and in St. Mary's Church, Bedford.   Large numbers of Saxon graves, the bodies mostly laid north and south (each with a knife at the waist) have been found at Chalton, and many have been found on the heath at Leighton Buzzard.   At Toddington large numbers of spearheads, helmets, shields, brooches, beads, and other ornaments have been found. Part of a Saxon shield has been found at Totternhoe. The remains of Saxon jars are to be met with in the fields all over the Dunstable district.   The swords, daggers, helmets, and shields of the Saxons were of iron, as this metal soon perishes under oxidation Saxon arms are generally found in a more or less imperfect state.   To preserve them, when found, from further and utter destruction, they should be carefully made red-hot and dropped into hot or boiling linseed oil, this will permanently arrest any further oxidation.

The late Dr. Edward Lawford had a collection of local Anglo-Saxon antiquities at Leighton Buzzard, and the late Major W. C. Cooper, F.S.A., a second and much larger collection at Toddington Manor House.

The former presence of the Danes near Dunstable is suggested by such names as Dane-end,

The Coming of the Danes.
near Luton; Dagnall, Danesborough, Ravensbury, Baldock, Thunder-dell, near Ashridge, and Tewin; but further research and spade-work is needed.   Dagnall appears to be equivalent with Daga's hall. A sister of our Queen is named Dagmar, the

feminine form of Daga. The Danish pronunciation is Dawgnall. The meaning of Danesborough seems obvious. Ravensbury may have been taken from the sacred bird of the Danish standards, the raven. Baldock may be founded on Balder, or Baldur, the sun-god. Thor, or Thunor, may be commemorated in Thunder-dell and Thunridge, Herts; and the god Tiw, or Tew, in Tewin, Herts. Outside the Dunstable district, on the east, there are many place-names of apparently Danish origin.

Alfred the Great (A.D. 871-901), in his contests with the invading Danes, forced them back from the neighbourhood of Dunstable to the agreed boundary-line from London to Leagrave by the Lea, and from Leagrave to Bedford by road through Flitwick to Bedford. The Danes were on the east of this local boundary, and the Saxons on the west. The Midland Railway from Leagrave to Bedford is practically on this old boundary line. But when Alfred's son, Edward the elder, came to the throne, in 901, the Danes raided over the boundary-line into Mercia. Near this boundary-line, to the south, stood Dunstable. As the site of the boundary between Saxon and Dane was close to where Dunstable now is, it follows that sword-and-knife work, and fire, were locally chronic during Saxon and Danish times; so that when William the Conqueror's messengers came to where Dunstable now is, in 1086, to compile Domesday Book, they found it completely wiped out.

Evidence of violent death is often visible in British Saxon and Danish bones. I have recently described and illustrated a British skull from the Lea. The man who once owned the skull died from two severe blows on the top of the head from a metal dagger; the first blow badly bruised and depressed the bone, but was ineffectual; the second completely dislodged a piece of the frontal bone, and crashed right through into the brain. When found, the piece of loose bone was inside the skull.

A few years ago I disinterred a number of Saxon skeletons at Chalton; one of these, with a knife at the waist, had only one leg; the leg had been removed at

the hip, out of the acetabulum of the pelvis.　How this
fellow entirely lost one leg one can only surmise, but it
is certain that he was buried with one only.　In those
days doctors, when existant, could not set limbs or deal
with serious wounds.　If a man got a leg broken or
torn out of the socket, he would have to hop about **on**
one leg for the rest of his days, if he happened to
recover.

The nearest place that survived the Dane was
Houghton and what remained of Saxon Dunstable was
probably a mere outlying market or staple, really belonging to Houghton.　As there was already a market at
Houghton, the Dunstable position was probably known
as the outlying market, Dun-staple, or the hill market-
place, in reference to the adjoining Downs.　Houghton
had not yet become Houghton Regis, Sælig Houghton,
fortunate Houghton.

CHAPTER VI

The Coming of the Normans.

ONE of the first glimpses we get of the neighbourhood of Dunstable in Norman times is in Domesday Book, which contains the Great Survey of Britain, ordered by William the Conqueror in 1086. Nearly all the towns and villages round Dunstable are **Domesday Book.** mentioned with the names of the owners of the different properties, and a list of the human beings, oxen, swine, ploughs, etc., on the different farms. Some of the present day villagers still bear the identical Saxon or Norman names, as Odel and Lewin, borne by the farmers of the time of William the Conqueror. The local place-names of the time of William the 1st are usually not quite the same as those at present in vogue, sometimes they are very different, and this shows the futility of guessing at the possible meaning of any present day names. The original sources must in every case, where possible, be got at. Caddington is Cadendone in Domesday, the first means Cædda's town, the latter Cædda's Hill. Toddington is Dodingtone, the family name being different. Battlesden is Battlesdone, the first a valley the second a hill. Biscot is Bissoppescote. Chalgrave is Celgrave. Studham is Estodham. Edlesborough is Edingeberge. Flitton—someone's town, is Flicteham, and becomes someone's home. Harrowden, meaning a certain hollow, is Herghetone, a town. Hockliffe a cliff, is Hockleia, a place. The modern rustic pronunciation " Hockley " is correct.

Houghton is Houstone.   Kensworth is Canesworde.
Leighton is Leston. Luton, Loitone. Milton is Middle-
tone. Tilsworth is Pileworde, on a Norman French
monument in the Church it is Tullesworth. Shillington
is Sethlingdone, instead of being a town it is a hill of a
clan. Tingrith is Tingrei. Stanbridge is Stanburge, a
stone-fort replaced in name by a modern non-existent
stone bridge; the older village folk, however, still
correctly say Stanburg.

The accompanying photographic reproduction of the
Domesday entry for the little village of Sewell will give
a good idea of the nature of the old writing, of what is
said in the entries, and how the words are abbreviated.

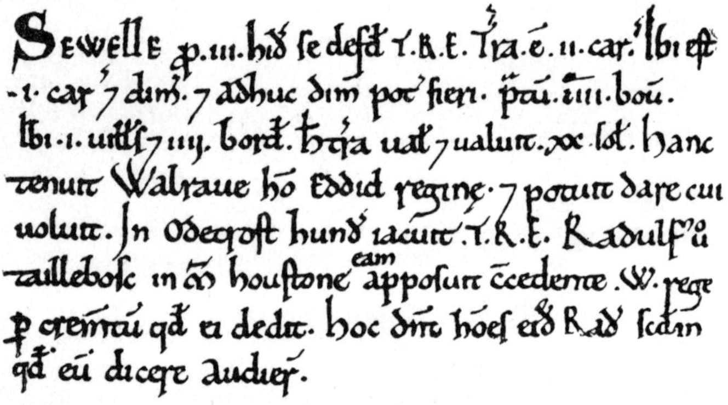

Fig. 12.   FAC-SIMILE FROM DOMESDAY BOOK OF ENTRY FOR
SEWELL. SIZE OF ORIGINAL

In modern type-letters this abbreviated Latin reads as
follows, printed line for line :—

SEWELLE, p. iii. hid se deft T.R.E.   Tra. e. ii. car.   Ibi est
i. car et dim & adhuc dim pot fieri.   Pat iiii. bov.
Ibi i. vills & iiii. bord.   H tra vat & vat & valuit. xx sol. Hanc
tenuit Walrave ho Eddid regine & potuit dare cui
voluit.   In Odecroft hund jacuit. T.R.E.   Radulf vo
Taillebosc in M Houstone eam apposuit ccedente. W. rege
p cremtu qd ei dedit. Hoc din hoes ejd Rad. scdm
qd eu dicere audier.

When the missing letters are added, the extended reading is as follows, printed line for line:—

Sewelle pro iii hidis se defendebat tempore Regis Edwardi. Terra
    est ii carucarum.   Ibi est
i caruca et dimidium et adhuc dimidium potest fieri.   Pratum
    iii. bovis.
Ibi i villanus et iiii bordarii.   Hæc terra valet et valuit xx solidos.
    Hanc
tenuit Walrave homo Eddid reginæ et potuit dare cui
voluit.   In Odecroft hundredo jacuit tempore Regis Edwardi
    Radulfus vero
Taillebosc in Manerio Houstone eam apposuit concedente Willelmo
    rege
per crementum quod ei dedit.   Hoc dicunt homines ejusdem
    Radulfi secundem
quod eum dicere audierunt.

Translation.

Sewell vouched for 3 hides in the time of King Edward.   There is land for 2 ploughs, and yet another half may be made.   Meadow for 4 oxen.   There is 1 villain and 4 bordars.   The land is and was worth 20 shillings.   Walrave a man of Queen Edith held this, and could give it to whom he wished.   It lay in Odecroft Hundred in the time of King Edward but Ralph Taillesbosc placed it in the Manor of Houghton, King William granting the same for an increased rent.   The men of the same Ralph say this is according to what they have heard him say.

Explanation of Terms Used.

Hide = An uncertain and variable number of acres, supposed to
            be 120—sufficient for the work of one plough.
Ploughs = Plough-teams—*carucarum*—four oxen to a team.
King Edward = Edward the Confessor.   Queen Edith = wife and
    survivor of the Confessor.
Villain = An important and typical tenant in villainage or serfdom,
            who usually held a quarter hide or virgate of land
            —30 acres.
Bordars = Cottage tenants, holding about five acres.
20 shillings = £30 present money.

Directly after the Domesday Survey was made we get a most interesting and instructive item of news from the pen of Matthew Paris, the thirteenth century monk of St. Albans. **The Miracle Play of St. Katherine.** The date of the birth of Matthew is unknown, but it is known that his death occurred in A.D. 1273.   The passage occurs in Matthew's *Lives of the First Twenty-three Abbots of St. Albans,* from the first Saxon abbot, Willigod, to the twenty-third abbot, John of Hertford.   The item occurs in the life of the sixteenth abbot, one Gaufrid, or Geoffrey, who was abbot for twenty-six years—from 1120 to 1146.

The event referred to is the presentation, at "Dunestaple" of the Miracle Play of St. Katherine, ten years or less before Gaufrid became abbot. If we say five years it gives us the date 1115—that is, twenty-nine years after the compilation of Domesday Book. The two events, however, might have been much nearer together as regards time. The play was performed from fifteen to thirty-five years before the foundation of Dunstable Priory by Henry I. The play could not, therefore, have taken place inside the church, or in the priory, as is so commonly stated. Matthew's record shows that Dunstable was already known as "Dunestaple" many years before the foundation of the town and priory by Henry I.

The following is a translation of the Latin description of the play, as printed in the *Vitæ viginti trium Abbatum Sancti Albani* :—"Matthæi Parisiensis Opera. Londini, 1640." I am not aware that this has ever been printed before, except in a newspaper report of an address of my own at Dunstable :—

"This abbot Gaufrid sprang from the good stock of the people of Caen, in Normandy ; and he was not only gifted with polite manners, but adorned with considerable knowledge of theology.* When the Abbot Richard died † he‡ received, albeit unwillingly, the election to the government of all the brethren of the church ‖, with the assent of King Henry I. of the English.

"So he came from Caen, whence he § sprang, being called by the Abbot Richard, whilst he was still a layman, that he might govern the school at St. Albans. But when he arrived the school had been given to another master, because he did not come in time. He lodged, therefore, at Dunestaple, awaiting the school of St. Albans, which had been repromised to him, where ¶ he instituted a certain festival of St. Katherine **, which we commonly call Miracles. For the celebration of which he asked that the choristers' capes †† might be lent, and

---

* *Divina scientia*.　　　† 1119.　　　‡ Gaufrid.
‖ St. Albans.　　§ Gaufrid.　　§ "legit."
¶ Dunstable.　** Sancta Katerina.　　†† cape chorales.

he obtained them, and the festival of St. Katharine took place. Now, it happened by chance on the following night that the house of Master Gaufrid took fire, and was burnt, with his books and the above-mentioned capes. Not knowing, therefore, in what way this loss to God and St. Alban might be restored, he gave himself up a whole offering to God by assuming the dress of religion in the House of St. Alban. And this was the cause why he exhibited such diligence, that afterwards being promoted in that same House as Abbot, he made precious choristers' capes."

The performance either took place in the open-air or in a small wooden church or school, with a thatched roof, possibly near to where Priory Road now is. The early church might indeed have been dedicated to St. Katherine, a minor saint, and the dedication changed to St. Peter, one of the greatest of saints by Henry I., for the new church.

The play represented the conversion and martyrdom of St. Katherine of Alexandria at a feast appointed by Maximianus II., in A.D. 305. St. Katherine is said to have discarded Jupiter for Christ. For this she was condemned to death on a revolving horizontal wheel. The wheel represented the Sun or Jupiter. After death the wheel was commonly upraised vertically with the martyr's body attached, as an offering to Jupiter, but in St. Katherine's case angels are asserted to have descended from heaven, and these by their mere presence caused the wheel to fall to pieces. One version of the story states that the maid was thereupon set free ; another that the martyr was beheaded and the body carried by angels to Mount Sinai, where it is still said to be preserved in the Convent of St. Katherine. Such was the plot of the Miracle Play performed by Dunstable rustics about the year 1115.

It is remarkable that the writer of these lines found at Dunstable in 1880, a 12th Century Seal, engraved with a representation of the Martyrdom of St. Katherine, in the finest style of 12th Century art. It was found near the north end of where Priory Road now is before houses were built, and near the site of the now vanished choir of the ancient church.   Fig. :—

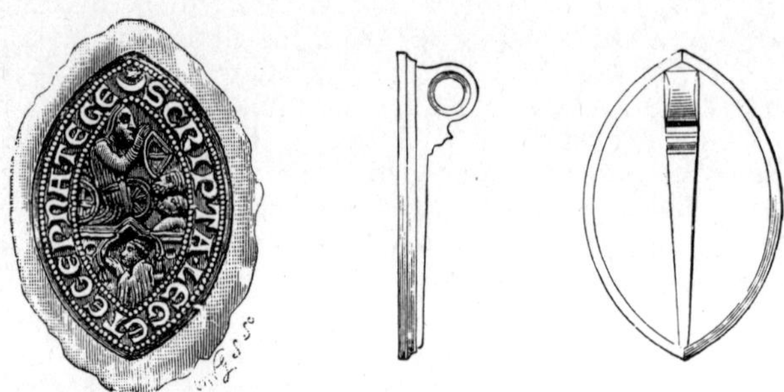

Fig 13.   SEAL, WITH REPRESENTATION OF THE MARTYRDOM OF ST. KATHERINE, ACTUAL SIZE.   *Now in the Collection of Sir John Evans, K.C.B.*

On the left is St. Katherine in the attitude of prayer, with the broken wheel of martyrdom.   On the right the faces of the Angels who descended from heaven. Beneath is a figure of the owner of the Seal in the attitude of prayer.   The legend is unusually clear and reads in a rhyming fashion—SCRIPTA . LEGE . TEGE . PNA . TEGE.   The fourth abbreviated word, PNA, is very puzzling, it was years before a satisfactory explanation presented itself in PN(EUM)A—spirit. The translation is— " Read what is written, the spirit conceal "—at first sight a dark saying, but it probably meant—" Read the writings, enclose the spirit in thy heart."   The Seal is unique in subject and legend, although rhyming legends of a similar class are frequent as—" Frange, lege, tege " —break, read, hide ; " tecta, lege, lecta, tege "—hide, read ; read, hide ; and " Scripta, lege, tege, verba, tege " —read the writings, hide, the words.   The word " hide " here always means enclose in thy heart.   See Folk Lore.

CHAPTER VII

The Norman Church of St. Peter, Dunstable.

THE documentary evidence for the date of the foundation of the Church and Monastery of Augustinian Canons is scanty.   In the *Annales Prioratus de Dunstaplia* no date is given by Richard de Morins, who was prior from 1202 to 1242.   In an entry before Richard's nomination it is, however, stated that Henry I. died in the year 1135, and that he founded the priories of Reading, Cirencester and Dunstaple.

Documentary Evidence as to Date.

In the charter granted to Dunstable by Henry I., the name of Robert de Bethune, bishop of Hereford, occurs as one of the witnesses.   Robert was consecrated in June, 1131.   The priory was therefore founded after this date and before the death of the king, in 1135. From a study of the names of the other witnesses, the date of the founding of the church is believed to be 1132.   The first sentence of the Charter of Henry I. states that the charter was given by the king to the church of " the Blessed Peter at Dunestapel."

The *Annales* state that it was not till eighty-one years after the granting of the charter, in 1132, viz., in 1213, that the buildings were sufficiently advanced by the Augustinian canons, for the dedication of the church to St. Peter, by Bishop Hugh II. of Lincoln.

The *Annales* state that in 1220 the great altar of the
Holy Cross and all Angels, and a second
The Progress altar of St. John the Baptist, were dedi-
of the cated by Robert Bishop of Lismore. An
Buildings. altar of St. Mary was dedicated by Hugh,
Bishop of Ely, in 1231. These dates are of great value,
and show that the nave, choir, transepts, and Lady
Chapel were practically completed by 1231. An entry
under 1222 states that two Norman towers belonging to
the west front, and the roof of the Presbytery, fell in
a great storm; these towers must not be confounded
with the present belfry, which is of much more recent
date. In 1228 St. Mary's Chapel was founded; in 1324
it was pulled down and entirely rebuilt. In 1250 an
inner gate within the court was built, and in 1251 a new
dormitory, to replaee an old one then in a dangerous
state, and a new stable was erected in 1257. In 1273
the body of the church was restored. New bells were
given in 1277, a new body to the bakehouse, and the
brewhouse wall, were built in 1282, a clock placed over
the *pulpitum*, or choir-screen, in 1283. In 1289 two
pinnacles were built on the north front of the church,
and the roof of the north porch was restored. The
great cross, and many figures of saints, were repainted
in 1293. In 1349 a new bell was added to the belfry.
These dates show that the church and monastic buildings, with the internal furnishing, required more than
150 years for their erection, completion, and partial
restoration after accidents from storms, and from the
after-effects of bad construction. The majority of the
buildings are not mentioned in the *Annales*, or, if
mentioned, only by empty names, as the " prior's house,"
the " chapter-house," etc. The juxtaposition of some of
the buildings is indicated by such entries as the one of
1222, where it is stated that one of the two western
towers fell on to the prior's hall. The prior's hall must
therefore have adjoined the south-western tower. The
other tower fell on to the stone roof of the church, which
it shattered.

It is usual to describe the exterior before the interior
of a church. The oldest part of the exterior is the

great western portal with the large semi-circular arch. It is of Transitional Norman age, and the date is about A.D. 1215. The right hand and more ornamental half of the pointed arch flush with the wall

The Great Western Portal. to the left and the smaller interlaced arches, without columns, just below are of the same date. The capitals of the north door are also of this age, the arch above the north door is modern. The whole of the filling within the great arch is much later in date than the arch and jambs. The filling was built in about A.D. 1450, to prevent the large arch from dropping in. It will be observed that no columns are present to support the eight capitals, these have dropped away, some were plain, others were ornamented with plait work, pieces of the plain examples may be seen built into the boundary wall on the right; other pieces ornamentally carved are on the rockwork in the Priory field. Two carved busts, in fairly good condition were to be seen over the two outermost capitals, fifty or sixty years ago, these were traditionally said to be portraits of Henry I. and his queen, on the northern bust the face, hair, and crown of the king were distinct. The carving of the capitals as well as those of the north door are worthy of close attention as fine examples of thirteenth century art. There are four series or orders of carving in the great arch, each order starting from the abacus or cover moulding of a capital. The first or outer order is preceded by fine zig-zag work facing outwardly and inwardly, next is a series of interlacing ovals resembling links of a large chain. In alternate links there were—one can hardly say there are—figures of angels with outspread wings, and the hands placed together in the attitude of prayer. The busts of the king and queen were in front of the links designed for the first angels above the capitals. The angels at the top of the arch meet head to head and are (or were) separated by a key-stone of carved foliage. The alternate links were filled with carved foliage radiating from the centre of the arch. The second order was carved with repetitions of infant faces, each face surrounded by small conventional wings, the carvings

F

Drawn by]   *Norman and Early English Doorways, Dunstable Priory Church.*   [The Author.

represented cherubim and each face, one on every stone of the arch, unlike the angels, radiated from the centre. The third tier was like the first, a series of interlaced ovals. The interior of the links was alternately foliage

Arcading on the West Front of Dunstable Priory Church, showing the junction of the Norman and Early English Masonry.

and small figures, the latter belonging to Bible history, in some instances there were two figures within a link. The fourth and inner series also consisted of ovals containing alternate figures and foliage, but in this instance the ovals were not linked. The figure subjects of some of the capitals may be made out—on one is a representation of St. David with a harp. The figures with long scrolls probably represent prophets or evangelists with their writings. This Transitional Norman work is of the finest class of its date.

The Early English work. A.D. 1220-1250. To this period of art the fine pointed door of the tower belongs, the seven niches above, and the fine open gallery of nine open arches extending from the tower to the great portal. No doubt the townsfolk were sometimes addressed by the clergy from this gallery. The gallery has lately—1903—been entirely removed and replaced with new work. The five small niches above are Early English work. The northern and southern buttresses and the lower tier of the turret are also Early English, the finest of its class. The niches over the pointed tower door were designed for figures, all of which have been destroyed—the pedestals alone remain. A series of figures also occupied the niches on the great buttress, but all have now vanished.

The Perpendicular work. A.D. 1450. The filling of the great doorway, including the square-headed doorway and the semi-circular filling above with the three niches for figures, belong to this date. The three figures which once occupied the niches have been destroyed. The belfry with the upper part of the staircase turret and the battlement from the tower to the southern turret are Perpendicular work. This Perpendicular work of the church is of a high class.

The northern aisle is modern, it formerly ended one bay short of its present length to the east. The new work was executed in 1876, and a bay added to form a vestry. The old, formerly external, restored eastern window of this aisle is now inside the Church, and separates the back of the organ from the vestry. Most of the so-called Perpendicular work of the North Aisle, before 1850, was of the basest and worst executed class. It was shored up for several years, and then practically fell from its bad workmanship. It was during the restoration in 1876 that the northern door was brought to light. It is common to find the northern door of churches built up in the Dunstable district. Before Reformation times the sexes separated in the churchyard; the males entered by the south door and the females by the north; the females sat on the north side of the interior and the males on the south. The worshippers left the church by the doors through which they entered and rejoined in the churchyard. At Dunstable the southern side of the church was occupied with cloisters, so the males entered by the south-west door, now built up. After the Reformation the sexes were not separated, and the north door, which admitted the cold north wind, was filled up with masonry. The south side of a churchyard, being sunny and warm, was always the favourite for burials; the north side being cold and in shadow, was less approved. The more ancient tombs are usually found at the east end of the churchyard, this place having been selected for its close proximity with the altar within the church.

The entire Nave is Norman, and dates from 1150 to **The Interior.** 1200. Older work dating from 1132, or soon after, once existed at the east end, but the oldest work was destroyed at the demolition of the religious houses. The eastern end of the nave and the lower great columns and arches are the older, the triforium above the nave arches the newer. There was originally a walk along the triforium from east to west, on both sides, the present fillings of the triforium arches are modern imitations of Perpendicular work. Originally there was another tier of arches, or clerestory, but this has vanished. Whether the original roof was of stone or wood is uncertain, the present roof is modern. The side chapel at the east end of the south aisle is modern or practically so, the two next bays south of the iron rail are Norman; the three western bays are new, or imitation-Norman. The unworked blocks of stone in the nave capitals are modern. The gallery at the west end is Early English and fine work of its class.

The filling in of the arch under the south side of the tower is (or was) Perpendicular. Restorers are now at work upon it. Till 1903 there was a good Perpendicular

Photograph]   **West Front, Dunstable Priory Church.**   [H. A. Strange.

door in this side of the filling with pedestals above for two figures. The two figures were destroyed long ago with other figures. The eastern filling was put in some time after 1670. This is now in course of removal.

The lower part of the present east wall represents the *pulpitum*, or choir-screen, which separated the people's church from the old choir. Originally it was not much higher than the top of the present hangings, it was only carried to the roof after the demolition of religious houses; the upper part of the wall was made up of stones, many richly carved, of the destroyed buildings. Originally there was a large central door in this wall, behind where the present altar stands—it can be clearly seen outside the church; but in the fourteenth century this central opening was filled in, and two smaller doors made right and left of the present altar for access to the choir. The present altar stands on the site of the great ancient altar of the Holy Cross and all Angels. At the time of the alteration the niches were made which still exist right and left of the altar. The niche on the south contained a figure of St. Mary, as shown by the monogram still remaining. The one on the north probably either contained a figure of St. John, or of the archangel Gabriel. There was also a large central niche, which must have contained a figure of the Lord. If Gabriel was the northern figure the composition represented the Annunciation, with the Lord in Glory, like the group in the Chantry of Henry V. at Westminster, where the two figures of St. Mary and St. Gabriel still remain. The group might, however, have represented the Crucifixion, with St. John and St. Mary. All the figures have been destroyed. The doorways and niches were originally furnished with canopies. It is obvious, then, that the base of the present eastern wall was, first a choir-screen with a central door; next, a rood-screen, with two side-doors and three niches. It was probably furnished above with a large rood or figure of the crucified Lord. When the choir was demolished, the rood was destroyed, and the base of the wall built upon to make an eastern wall. At this latter time, therefore, there was temporarily no rood-screen. The present wooden screen is a newer chancel-screen, and it dates from the end of the fourteenth century. It was removed at an uncertain date from the east to the west end of the church and placed up in front of a modern organ-gallery. During the last restoration it was again removed from the west to the east.

The incongruous pulpit is modern, the font is a modern imitation of a Norman font which existed prior to 1850. The flamboyant painting on the east wall is, of course, modern.

I remember the church well at this date. I was then studying for the profession of archi-**The Church prior to 1850.** tecture. I was a zealous student, and measured and drew all parts of the building. The church was entered by the main door over a stone coffin ; an organ gallery filled the westernmost bay of the Nave. At right and left under this gallery were wooden staircases for the organist, bellows-blower, the scholars of Chew's school, and men and women of the choir ; the women were in front, and the men separated behind. Two pews were claimed as seats by a few worshippers. The spaces between the Nave-arches at the south-west were ornamented with paintings of Norman date, and the mouldings of the arches were also painted with zigzag ornaments.

The font was on the right of the central passage ; on the left, on the floor, was a stone coffin, and on the first Norman pier, on the left, was a holy-water stoup, over which was carved a stone angel with outspread wings. In the first bay of the north aisle, upon a sill, was a large, old-fashioned hour-glass and a knight's helmet. A modern man with a big skull once put his head into this helmet, and had great difficulty in getting it out again ; he could not regulate the back of his head so as to clear his chin. This helmet probably formed part of the arms of the " very famous squire " who was killed in a tournament at Dunstable and buried in the Priory in April, 1293. The arms were formerly in the possession of a " Mr. Cole," of Dunstable, according to the *Bibliotheca Topographica Britannica*, vol. iii. p. 193. There

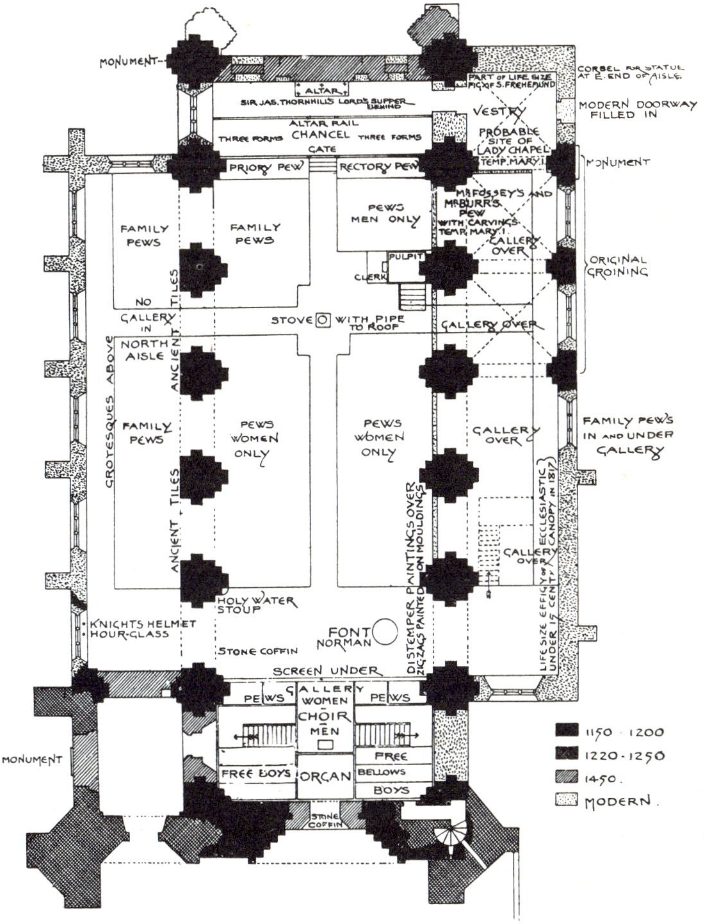

Drawn by]   The Author.

Plan of Dunstable Priory Church in the year 1850.

were ancient tiles below, and grotesque heads carved in stone above. The north aisle contained so-called "family pews." The bulk of the nave was reserved for women, but there were "family pews" towards the east end on the left, and pews for "men only" on the right. The Elizabethan wooden pulpit and sounding-board were on the right, attached to the pier which is now touched by the screen. In the middle of the church, and a little west of the pulpit, was a stove with a black iron pipe which passed right through the roof. The altar-rail stretched north and south from the two first free piers from the east; on the left, west of the rail, was the "Priory pew," on the right, the "Rectory pew." There were six forms east of the rail, in two groups of three each, north and south. Behind the small holy-table was the fine large picture of "The Last Supper," by Sir James Thornhill. Right and left of this picture were paintings of Moses and Aaron with the Ten Commandments beneath. There were ancient wooden stalls, or *misereres*, the seats of which could be turned up; the under sides were carved with figure subjects. The south aisle, on entering from the great door, presented the stairs to a wooden gallery which occupied four of the Norman bays. The pews in and under the gallery were termed "family pews." Beyond the back of the pulpit were the pews of Mr. Burr and Mr. Fossey, ornamented with the fine carvings, some of which are now placed over a wooden screen on the south side of the vestry. At the end of the south aisle, at that time the vestry, on the floor, was a damaged life-size stone figure of St. Frehemund, and a corbel stood out from the wall, designed for a statue. There were many stone coffins and brasses in the nave and aisles. In the earlier restorations, no proper respect was paid to any of the objects above enumerated, or to the bones of the dead. The old pulpit was sold by auction in the market-place. A scaffold-pole was put through Thornhill's picture, and it has now been rolled up in the church tower for many years. Anyone who liked could take a brass or a piece of old carving. In this way the knight's helmet and hour-glass were lifted.

Some of the best remaining brasses have been from **The Brasses.** 1851 to now, kept loose amongst unworthy surroundings in the church chest. A few stone carvings are in the Priory grounds, others elsewhere. A small number of objects have been restored to the church. Prior to the first restoration stones were dug up out of the site of the old choir for local purposes, a schoolmaster collected a large number of richly carved stones and kept them in his house and garden. At his death they were carted to and buried on the downs near Whipsnade turning at a spot marked on the map. In a shed in the town, generally occupied by a bull, is some kind of stone vessel from the church, apparently made of alabaster. It can be felt rather than seen and has been seemingly used as a pig trough. One of the stone coffins was used as a horse trough in the field south-west of the town, where marked on the map. An inscribed bell, said to be the old Sanctus Bell, is used as a fire-bell. The superb carvings on the south of the vestry were thrown into the churchyard and left unguarded; some were used for fires. The angel over the holy-water stoup and the stoup itself were destroyed. In 1817 there existed in the wall at the west end of the south aisle a fine recumbent effigy of an ecclesiastic under a carved fifteenth century canopy. There is a steel engraving of the monument in Fisher's *Collections for Bedfordshire*. Not a fragment now remains in the church. I saw the canopy dug out of the cellar of the public-house at the corner of West Street in 1885. It was Christmas time, and I was passing on my way to the Railway Station for London. On my return the carved stones had all been removed, I was told, to Leighton Buzzard.

The vestry of Dunstable Church is separated from the chancel on the north side by a **Marian Wood Carvings in the Church.** wooden screen, surmounted by wooden columns or banisters—one large and eight small. These columns are of unusual archæological interest, and of great excellence. Before 1850 there was a second large column, the lower half of which has lately been restored to the church;

Photograph]   **Screen and Chancel, Dunstable Priory Church.**   [*J. Field.*

the upper half was burnt as fuel. There was also a canopy, and other work now quite lost ; some was used for fire-wood.

At the time of the Dissolution of the Religious Houses every piece of symbolical carving found in the church was completely destroyed, so that it is certain that if these fragile wood carvings had then existed they would not have been left intact. The carvings are symbolical of the death of the Lord, of St. Mary, and the house of St. Augustine. The date of the work is that of the reign of Queen Mary, soon after the death of Henry's young son Edward VI. In other words, the date is from 1553 to 1558. Edward VI. was a Protestant, and no such work would have been executed during his reign. Mary, the daughter of Katherine of Aragon, was, on the contrary, a zealous Catholic, and it was in her time that the carvings were executed. During the strongly Protestant times of Queen Elizabeth— Henry's daughter by Anne Boleyn—the execution of such work would, again, have been impossible.

It is well known that Queen Mary laboured hard to support and re-establish the Roman Church, to restore the old churches destroyed in the time of her father, and to found new Roman establishments, as at Greenwich, Sion, and Sheen. She probably attempted to restore Dunstable during the tenure of the first two Protestant rectors, Robert Russell and John Cooper. Queen Mary seems to have had this work made for a Lady Chapel, to replace the old Lady Chapel desecrated, as she thought, by Cranmer, who declared within the old building, at the divorce of Katherine, that Mary was base-born and illegitimate. The archbishop, as is well-known, was at last burnt at Mary's order.

An enumeration of some of the beautifully carved symbols will indicate the nature of the work—Lily, crossed swords, flaming heart, the two pierced hands of Jesus, the crown of thorns, the money-bag of Judas, the lash of the scourging, a castle, a portcullis, a pome-granate, a fir-cone, a sun, an hour-glass, a double rose, an anchor, a double-headed eagle, a grave-digger's mat-tock, a feather, the ladder of the cross, the lantern of the Mount of Olives, a rosary, the pincers of the Cruci-fixion, the nails, a centre-bit, a hammer, and the face of the Lord. Other carvings, burnt in recent times, represented the Lord's tunic, a bleeding heart, crossed palm-branches, the pierced feet of the Lord, the column and cord of the scourging, the vine, the hand of Judas clutching the money-bag, a Roman spear, and the dice of the Roman soldiers. Prior to 1850 the carvings, with a canopy and other work, formed a large pew at the east end of the south aisle.

At the west end of the interior of the church are three wooden shelves, each 5 ft. 1 in. long, the **Mrs. Cart's Bread.** upper with a wooden tympanum. The shelves are, or rather were, for loaves of bread for weekly distribution to fifteen widow-recipients under the will of Mrs. Jane Cart, early in the eighteenth century. The woodwork dates from about this time. The shelves are in bookcase fashion. In times past the widows received the bread after each Sunday afternoon's service, but of late a different plan has been adopted.

CHAPTER VIII.

Relics formerly Preserved in Dunstable Church.

THE following legend of St. Frehemund was compiled long before the publication of the Rev. Canon Wood's "*Forgotten Saint*" in the *Antiquary* of 1893. I was assisted by the late Rev. Denis Murphy, S.J., LL.D., Vice-President of the Royal Society of Antiquaries of Ireland, and many other friends. The chief sources of the legend are both editions of Dr. Horstman's *Nova Legenda Angliæ* and Lydgate's Metrical Translation, Stadler's *Heiligen-Lexikon*, Father Stanton's *Menology of England and Wales*, under the Saints' Day, May 11th, Camden's *Warwickshire* and Leland's *Itinerary*. All available *Lives of Saints* published in this country and abroad have been consulted. For obvious reasons the following abstract is greatly condensed.

The life of St. Frehemund is scattered in fragments over lists of minor saints. He is described as the eldest son of Offa, king of Mercia, and his **The Bones of** death is set down for A.D. 866. His father **St. Frehemund.** is reputed to have had a palace at Offley, not far from Dunstable. Frehemund is described as a king and martyr. A heathen child, three years of age, is said to have been miraculously gifted with prophesy, and to have foretold the birth and ultimate martyrdom of Frehemund as a Christian. After the prophesy the child begged to be baptised, and then died suddenly.

Frehemund was born, so we are told, a pagan, at Offchurch, in Warwickshire, was converted to Christianity, and became a king of Mercia. Tired of a kingly life, he made his way to Cærleon, near Cardiff, and then to the banks of the Severn and Lundy Island. On his way to the island he was badly tossed for five days in a stormy sea. The island is said to have been only fit for evil spirits, but Frehemund lived there for seven years, subsisting on roots and wild fruits. At the latter part of this time, the savage, red-haired Danes ravaged England, and Offa sent to Lundy Island for his son to help him in repulsing the merciless invaders. It is stated that the Danes numbered 24,000, and Frehemund's followers only twenty-two; but, to the Danes, every one of Frehemund's men appeared as a thousand. The great battle took place at Radford, near Offchurch, and the pagans were utterly routed and destroyed. Frehemund, in gratitude, fell on his knees and thanked Christ for the marvellous victory. At this moment an apostate Christian follower, filled with envy, drew his long Saxon sword, and with one swoop struck off the head of the saint. This event, so we are told, took place in the middle of May, A.D. 866.

The blood of Frehemund spurted over the face of the **The Legend.** murderer, and the trunk and head fell to the ground. The murderer, now filled with remorse, fell on his knees and besought forgiveness from the martyr, whereon the head turned and forgave the apostate. We are now informed that the trunk of Frehemund erected itself, picked up the blood-stained head in the left-hand, and walked for three miles to Harborough. The headless walking body was followed by Frehemund's amazed attendants; the body was seen, so it is reported, to take its sword and plunge it into the earth. This act caused a miraculous spring of pure water to spurt from the ground, and at this spring the body of Frehemund knelt. It washed the blood from the neck, and cleansed the blood-stains from the face. Thus purified and rebaptised, the head and body rested in death on the ground, and the soul of Frehemund, king and martyr, ascended to heaven.

The startled followers raised the head and body and carried them to Offchurch, where the remains were placed in a shrine. They are said to have rested in the shrine for sixty-six years.   During these years we are told that miracles before the shrine were of constant occurrence: the dumb regained speech, the deaf regained hearing, the blind their sight, and the hopelessly crippled stood upright and walked ; travellers from a distance were directed to the spot by a marvellous illumination of the sky which shone over the saint's shrine.

In the year A.D. 932 three young and holy virgins—one dumb, the other deaf, and the third a cripple, dreamed an identical dream.   An angel descended from heaven whilst they were asleep, and requested them to remove the skeleton of Frehemund from Redic to Cropredy, near Banbury, in north Oxfordshire.   The holy virgins secured the bones, and apparently carried them off by hand, as one virgin is described as carrying the " holy head." They reached Cropredy, dug a grave, and prepared an alabaster tomb or shrine.   They were, however, over-taken by darkness, and foolishly left the bones exposed near the grave.   Next morning, on revisiting the site, the bones and shrine were gone, and a branch which the virgins had fixed in the ground as a guide over-night had grown into a large willow tree.

The bones were now practically lost in a large field, but in the earth they were still so potent for good that the meadow only produced beneficent herbs, beautiful flowers, and luxuriant pasture.   Any sick beast placed in the field immediately recovered from any ailment or distemper.

At this time there was a certain pilgrim at the Holy Sepulchre at Jerusalem, and he dreamed three times the same dream—that an angel descended from heaven, and directed him to go to Cropredy, and dig up St. Frehemund's bones.   The pilgrim was incredulous, whereon for this wickedness the angel pulled one of his arms out of joint, and requested him to start forthwith on a tramp from Jerusalem to Oxfordshire.   In this long journey he went two hundred miles out of his way— four hundred in all—so that he might secure an inter-view with the pope. After great toil, the pilgrim, it is said, reached Cropredy, and found the bones.   At the moment

G

of finding, the pilgrim's dislocated arm suddenly and spontaneously set itself with a jerk. The skeleton of the saint was still powerful for good, and miracles were again wrought, and the fame of the bones spread to every part of England. The story now says that after a time, and with the full permission and authority of the pope, the bones were taken to Dunstable.

That the supposititious bones of this dubious saint and king were really at Dunstable in 1203 is certain, for in the *Annales Prioratus de Dunstaplia* under this date, it is stated that the bones were in the church. The *Annales* further state that King John was present, and he was so delighted with the relics that he proclaimed a three days' fair for the town in May, the month of the saint's death. This May fair in honour of St. Frehemund is still celebrated.

The same *Annales* inform us that an altar to St. Frehemund was dedicated in 1207, and that at Easter, 1212, numerous miracles were wrought at Dunstable at the intercession of the saint. In 1272 we are again reminded of St. Frehemund and daily prayers in the church. In 1275 the clergy confess to have taken 100s. by weight, from the offerings at the shrine of the bones of St. Frehemund for other purposes than the honor of the saint.

Matthew Paris says, under 1257, that Henry III. was at St. Albans in that year, and in conversation with Matthew the king named all the " holy kings and martyrs of England "—there were eleven in all, and Frehemund was one.

Richard de Morins was prior, when the bones were brought to Dunstable. The fame of the miraculous bones had no doubt reached his ears, and Richard probably visited Cropredy and purchased or begged the bones. That he acquired some old bones of some sort, somewhere, seems certain.

At the dissolution of the religious houses the shrine and altar were doubtlessly destroyed and the miraculous bones thrown away. There was at that time a life-size figure of St. Frehemund in the church, carrying a crowned head in its hand, this figure was only partially destroyed, for some of the older folk of Dunstable can remember seeing it in the present church when they were young.

Each year the May fair returns with its swings, round-abouts, aunt Sallies, stilt walkers, tight-rope dancers, merry-go-rounds, wild beast shows, ginger-bread, nuts, and sweets. Each year brass bands and steam organs return, accompanied by happy shouting and loud boisterous laughing. This is the local commemoration of Frehemund, saint, king, and martyr, as fixed seven hundred years ago by King John.

This was another relic; under date, 1240, we read in the *Annales* that the Dunstable clergy "had **The Tunic of St. Hugh.** a dispute with John, the rector of Luton, and archdeacon of Oxford, about the tunic of St. Hugh, and for peace sake they gave him " all the tunic but one sleeve." The cutting up of the tunic and the retention of one miraculous sleeve is curious, but in the thirteenth century human skeletons and mummified saints, kings and martyrs were often served in the same way, the limbs were not only broken off and sold but they were frequently stolen, so great was the avidity for securing a portion of a "holy saint." The St. Hugh here mentioned was probably St. Hugh, of Grenoble and Lincoln, the builder of the choir and part of the transepts of Lincoln Cathedral.

At the Dissolution, the original Norman holy-water stoup was destroyed, but in Mary's time a new one **The Holy-Water Stoup.** was carved out of the substance of one of the Norman piers at the north-west of the church. During the rectorship of the Rev. Frederick Hose, the stones from which this stoup was carved were taken out and replaced by plain stones. The newer stoup was of the date and in the style of the wood carvings in the present vestry.

The Fayrey Pall, long lost to the town, is now restored and in charge of the rector of Dunstable. **The Fayrey Pall.** The pall is said to have been given to the Fraternity of St. John the Baptist, at Dunstable, by Henry Fayrey, who died in 1516. At the Dissolution of the Monasteries—1536 to 1540

—it was lost sight of, but was probably preserved by the Wingate family, owners of the Brotherhood house, till about 1642. After 1642 the pall was in the possession of one John Miller, of Dunstable. In 1812 it was in possession of the churchwardens, who prior to this date allowed the parishioners to use it at funerals for a charge of sixpence. After 1812 the permission was withdrawn, and the churchwardens would neither allow it to be used or even seen. They had got rid of it. In 1838 the pall was in the private possession of a Rev. G. O. Miller, and he raised money on it, by depositing it it as security for money with a Dr. Pemberton, of Sternfield, in Suffolk. As the Rev. Mr. Miller died without repaying the money he had borrowed, Dr. Pemberton kept it in his private possession for thirty years, and then restored it as a free gift to Dunstable, under the charge of the rector of that time, the Rev. F. Hose. When Mr. Hose died, in 1883, the pall was removed from the rectory house, where it had been kept and retained by a son of the rector, living at a distance for eight years. After the expiration of the latter term, in 1891, the town and church once more regained the possession of the pall

The pall was exhibited in London, many years ago, at an exhibition of ecclesiastical needlework at South Kensington. It was then photographed, and a small, indifferent wood engraving was prepared from the photograph and published in *Needlework as Art*, by the late Lady Marian M. Alford. The authoress only gives a few lines of description, and terms the work " Dunstable Pall. Property of Vicar of Dunstable—ex officio."

The pall belongs to the Flemish school of art, and is of fifteenth century date—about 1450. The names of Henry, Agnes, John and Mary Fayrey occur upon the pall, and upon the two ends are portraits of John and Mary Fayrey, the father and mother of Henry. The merchant's mark of John Fayrey is embroided on the pall. This John Fayrey was a member of the Mercers' Company in London, and the arms of the Mercers' Company occur upon the pall. Henry, the son, was a member of the Haberdashers' Company, and the arms

of this company are also quartered on the pall.   John
and Mary Fayrey are commemmorated by heads of St.
John the Baptist and Mary the mother of the Lord.
Mary is the patron saint of the ancient company of
Mercers, founded by Henry II.

Photograph]   **Part of the Fayrey Pall.**   [*J. Field.*
Representing the St. Mary Crowned.

The central part of the pall is rich old Florentine,
brocaded velvet, powdered with fine small loops of gold
and cut from the roll.   The small gold loops show the
velvet to be of Florentine origin.   The embroidery is
fixed on to a heavily fringed border of satin.

The figures on the pall are four representations of St. John the Baptist in the wilderness, and at the head and foot are figures of John and Mary Fayrey in the attitude of prayer, both facing the Baptist.   Close to the figures of the donors are their initials and merchant's marks.   The names occur at length below.   On the sides are twenty-seven figures of the Fayrey family, fourteen men and thirteenth women all standing and facing the Baptist.   The four shields of arms on the sides, belong to the Mercers' Company, one quartered with the Haberdashers' Company, with the motto—" *Serve and obey*," and two presumably belonging to the Fayrey family.   One of the shields includes a face of St. Mary crowned with an eastern crown and issuing from clouds, with the motto, " *Honor Deo*."   The merchant's mark is that of John Fayrey, as shown by the initials, I. and F., the cross is that of St. John the Baptist, and the two angular lines at the bottom represent the top of a rock, or possibly the wilderness, the meaning of the heart from which the cross springs is obvious.

As regards the style of art of the figure subjects and arms, it is of the highest excellence, both as regards drawing and execution.   The men and women represented on the pall are the living men and women of the time of Henry VI. and Edward IV.   The fine Fayrey brass, once in the church, was got rid of during one of the recent restorations.

Two somewhat similiar palls are preserved in London, one by the Fishmongers' Company, believed by the Officers of the Company to have been made by nuns in the reign of Elizabeth.   The other belongs to the Vintners' Company, and is almost identical in design with, but a little later in date than, the Dunstable example.

CHAPTER IX.

The Church and Priory in the Thirteenth Century.

THE present church is a mere fragment of the original. All that is left of the outside is the great semi-circular arch and jambs, with a strip on the left. Even the nave is deficient of the eastern bay. The clerestory, the whole of the roof and the aisles, except two bays, have vanished. With such a fragment it is almost impossible for anyone except a trained antiquary to realize what the original building was like. As will be seen from the accompanying plan where the existing parts are solid black and the demolished parts in outline, there is not much more than one-third of the length of the original church left. The present eastern piers did not end the old nave by one bay. The enlargement of the south-east pier, as seen outside, is mere casing of a later date. It is not a large pier for the support of the demolished tower. The west front was probably originally built with a great gable, but when the Norman towers fell the gable was knocked down. Originally there was a high-pitched roof to follow the line of the gable, the line of the original high-pitched roof of the north aisle can be seen in the belfry. There was probably a massive central tower in the style of St. Albans Cathedral, and Norman chapels, as shown on the plan. The supporting piers of the towers had staircases for access to the triforium and upper parts of the tower. The uneven surface of the ground still indicates the position of the choir, and the line of the quadrangular cloisters can still be plainly seen in the priory meadow. The prior's

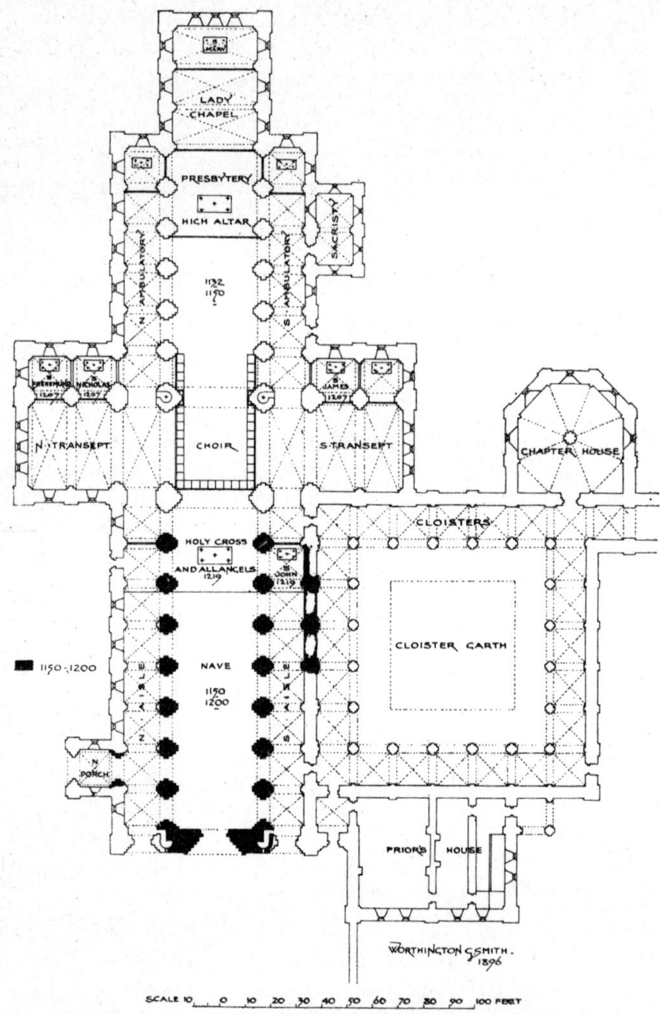

Drawn by]   [the Author.

The Augustinian Priory of St. Peter, Dunstable.
With conjectural restoration of Choir, Cloisters, Chapter House, etc.

house, the chapter house, the Lady chapel, the different altars, figures, etc., are mentioned by name and date in the *Annales Dunstaplia*. There can be no doubt that all the buildings belonging to the monastery were in the style of other Augustinian establishments, and included a long dormitory and refectory, an infirmary, school, guest house, *conversorium, scriptorium,* brewery, wine and beer cellars, kitchen, stables, barns, granaries, storehouses, etc., and houses for porters and servants. The cemetery was on the south-east of the presbytery. The king's house was where Kingbury House now is, and some of the massive foundations of the house still remain. In Norman times this was part of Houghton Regis. Until quite recent years there was a path from the north entrance of the church direct to the southern entrance of the king's house. The king's garden, several times referred to in old documents, was on the north side of Kingsbury House. Guests to the monastery were received at the guests' hall or *Hospitium* in the High Street, part of which now forms the ground floor of Messrs. Munt & Brown's factory. Its date is about A.D. 1300. The old way from the guest hall to the Prior's house and Monastic buildings can be clearly seen behind Messrs. Munt & Brown's warehouse, the trackway is popularly referred to as the roof of a subterranean passage.

The Monastic buildings were well drained, as far as surface water was concerned, by open drains, into pools where Dunstable Park now is. The first dry ditch bordered by the trees, in Britain Street, on the left from the High Street, and behind the houses in Priory Road is the beginning of the drain. It can easily be traced to Kingsbury, and through the farm buildings to the now dry Dunstable pond and the submerged part of Dunstable park. The drain is shown on the Map by a fine dotted line, near the more coarsely dotted footpath.

There were two public entrances to the monastery in **The Priory.** the thirteenth century—one at the guest hall, where Messrs Munt & Brown's factory now is, the other at the south-west corner of the church, where the ruined archway is. This archway, like Messrs.

Drawn by] **Conjectural Restoration of the Guest Hall of the Priory.** [the Author.
Now the drawing-room of a private house.

Munt & Brown's factory, is comparatively modern, and must not be confounded with the now demolished Norman entrance. The entrance near the church was entered by carriage or cart through a large semicircular Norman arch, with a small adjoining entrance for persons on foot, The entrance opened into a courtyard, with the prior's house on the left and a gate-house and porter's lodge on the right. The prior's house had an *auditorium*, or receiving room, on the ground floor, and a small chamber above, furnished with an *oratory* or small chapel with a stone altar. There was also a parlour and library of MSS.

On the south side of the church, and on the east of the prior's house, were cloisters, or open stone corridors with groined roofs, in the style of the aisles of the present church. These cloisters could be entered at the south-west angle of the church or from behind the prior's house. The cloisters formed a quadrangular walk, with two entrances to the church. Within the quadrangle was a grass plat, or *cloister garth* or lawn. The clergy walked and sometimes sat in the cloisters reading, writing, or studying in silence. A door opened from the cloisters into the chapter house and *scriptorium*. In the latter writings were made, and close by was a chamber for records. When the prior approached any of the sitting clergy they at once stood and bowed in silence as he passed. The silence was broken by music and singing, as the clergy not only practised these arts, but taught them in chambers set apart for teaching.

On the east of the cloisters was the *refectorium* or dining-hall, and near by the kitchen and cellars for beer and wine. No woman was ever seen in the kitchens or in any of the extensive priory buildings or grounds, for not only were women forbidden to enter, but the clergy were requested not even to look at the fair sex, either in the church, the streets, or the fields. Near the refectory was a garden and orchard, in which plants, roots, and fruits were grown. At meal-times the clergy trooped in a silent procession to the dining-hall, headed by the prior or sub-prior; they took their places at long tables, and stood in silence till grace had been said and repeated.   Each canon then made the sign of the cross on his forehead, and sat down in silence to the repast.   The food was served by men and boys, and signs, not words, were used for any wants.   The inmates were not allowed to consume food outside the refectory. During the meal one of the clergy read selections from the Gospels.   After the meal the canons retired to teach, read, write, or officiate in some service in the church.

Near the *refectorium* was the *infirmitorium*—a building erected for aged and sick " brothers."   The ailing were attended by doctors, surgeons, and nurses, all of the male sex.   Near the infirmary was a chapel dedicated to St. Martin.   The convalescent brothers walked and sat in the garden or orchard, mostly in silence ; all necessary speaking was briefly carried on in low tones. Speaking in an ordinary tone of voice was restricted to services in the church or for times of emergency.   An alarm bell was kept for cases of accident, fire, or attempted robbery.

The *dortor*, or dormitory, was a long chamber on the first floor, in which the canons slept.   The ground floor was termed the dortor basement ; the beds were arranged side by side and opposite, as in the wards of a hospital. The beds were held in common ; no one in the monastery had a right to anything—even clothes, every-thing belonged to the church.   A vow of total relinquish-ment of all earthly goods was made, put into writing, and laid before God on the altar, before entrance to the brotherhood could be gained.   In the dormitory were tables, bibles, prayer-books, candles, a clock, bell, and lantern, and suspended from the walls were the rules of the priory.

None of the clergy were allowed to sleep out of the dormitory.   When the clergy reached the dormitory, each knelt by the side of his bed whilst the sub-prior read prayers.   After prayers the canons undressed, made the sign of the cross, and retired to rest.   One of the clergy, however, sat up and watched during the entire night to see that all was right and orderly and to give alarm upon any sudden emergency.   Watchmen were also present in different parts of the Priory buildings and

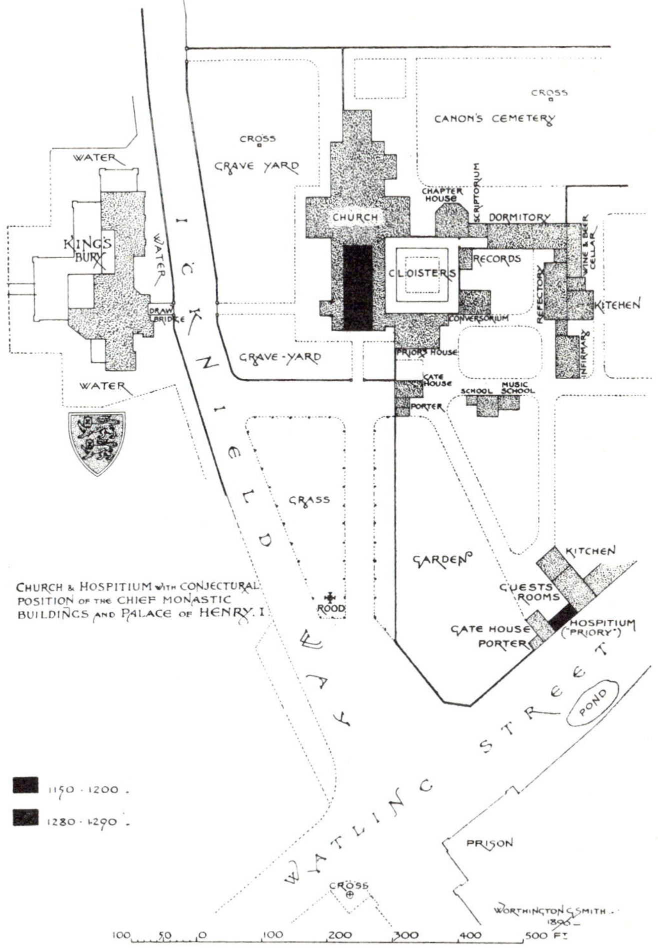

Showing the Hospitium with the conjectural positions of the Monastic Buildings
and the Palace of Henry I.

in the church.   Precisely at midnight a bell was loudly struck in the dortor to wake the canons; each of the clergy. thereupon sat up in bed, made the sign of the cross on the forehead, knelt in prayer at the bedside, and dressed.   Headed by the prior or sub-prior and a "brother" carrying a lantern, the clergy proceeded, in midnight darkness, from the dortor through the windy, cold, open eastern corridor of the cloisters, into the south aisle of the church, which they reached at a position now destroyed, but immediately behind the present western wall of the church.   The deep darkness of the church was only relieved by the sanctuary lamps before the altars.   These lamps were kept perpetually burning. The clergy proceeded to the high altar which once existed in the now destroyed presbytery.   The service was matins.   After the service the prior and canons profoundly bowed to the altar, re-formed in silent procession, and retraced their way through the eastern cloister corridor to the dortor.   Here they once more stood by their beds and undressed; they were not allowed to sit on the bed.   They knelt in prayer, made the sign of the cross, and retired again, in darkness and silence, to rest.   At the time appointed for rising for the work of the day the bell again sounded, the clergy again sat up in bed, crossed themselves, arose, prayed, dressed themselves, and washed at a large stone lavatory. Before breakfast, and before any duty of the day was entered upon, another service of the church was attended.   "There," the book of "Augustinian Obser-vances" states, "after sprinkling themselves with holy water, let them pray with pure hearts, fervently, and first seek the kingdom of God and his righteousness."

As the clergy trooped from the dortor to the church, they passed the entrance to the chapter house.   There every morning after breakfast the prior, sub-prior, and canons assembled to arrange the day's work.

The work of the day included more than writing, reading, and praying, as the garden and orchard had to be seen to; the cooking, brewing, and baking had to be attended to; the washhouse and laundry had to be looked after, carts mended, horses shod, and the tailoring and shoemaking seen to. Men and boys stood at the wash-tubs, and hung the garments to dry. A brother might be dead; a coffin had to be made and a grave dug in the cemetery. The burial-ground was near where the newer houses have been built in the Priory Road. Business had to be transacted out of doors, messengers sent to Caddington, Kensworth, Totternhoe, Houghton, Sewell, and other places. Sheep, shepherds, wool, wood, corn, roots, etc., all had to be looked after. Letters had to be written and guests received. It must not be supposed that the clergy themselves did washing, tailoring, and shoemaking; they supervised this work within the Priory buildings. All work was done with as little noise as possible; silence and implicit obedience were guiding rules of Augustinian conduct.

In the thirteenth century the church was nearly three **The Church.** times its present length, and one-third higher than now. It was much darker than at present, as the Norman windows were small, narrow, and filled with painted glass. There were no windows in the nave above the arches, as now. The present nave windows represent the open *triforia* of old, covered with high-pitched aisle roofs. The arches and spaces between, as well as the roof, which was probably of wood, were painted with ornaments and scriptural subjects. There was no pulpit or lectern in the nave, there were no pews. During service the worshippers knelt, and the preacher addressed his congregation from the steps of the altar. The air was generally laden with the odour of incense. The perpetually burning lamps before the numerous altars were suspended by long chains from the roof. The altar in the nave was dedicated to the Holy Cross and All Angels; in one of the aisles was an altar to St. John, in the transepts altars to St. Nicholas, St. James, and St. Frehemund. The high altar was in the Presbytery beyond, with altars right and left. There was probably an altar to St. Katherine. Beyond the high altar was the Lady chapel, with an altar to St. Mary. On the south of the presbytery was the sacristy, where the sacred vessels of the church were kept. The building was in charge of custodians night and day, not only to guard the treasures and relics of the church, but to watch for the expected coming of the Lord, as "a thief in the night." When services were held in the presbytery, the canons sat in stalls in the choir; at the times when the prior approached or passed they rose to their feet.

There is an impression of the priory seal at Westminster Abbey and several examples are in **The Priory Seal.** the British Museum. They are all more or less imperfect. There is a photograph of the seal and counter-seal taken from a British Museum example in the town hall, Dunstable. The seal is that of the prior named William de Wederow, or Wederhore, A.D. 1280-1302, attached to a charter of Pope Martin IV., A.D. 1283. The seal is two and a-half inches in diameter, and represents St. Peter seated on a throne with his right hand raised in benediction, and in the left hand two keys. The legend is " SIGILLVM ECCLESIÆ SANCTI PETRI DE DUNSTAPLE " (Seal of the Church of St. Peter, Dunstable). The counter-seal is a small pointed oval, 1 in. by 1⅝ ins. The subject is a double niche, with trefoiled arch, crocketed and having a turret between them. On the left is a king, crowned, holding an indistinct emblem; on the right, St. Peter. In the base, under a trefoiled arch, the prior is represented, half-length, in prayer. The legend is " SIGILLVM WILLELMI PRIORIS DE DUNSTAPLE " (Seal of William, prior of Dunstable).

The charter to which this seal is attached is an award made under a mandate from pope Martin IV., by the abbot of St. James-without-Northampton and the priors of St. Albans and St. Andrews, Northampton, in composition between the prior of St. Peter's, Dunstable, and Lawrence, abbot of La Dale, Stanley, Derby, respecting tithes in Bradshaw, or Bradwell, High Peak, Derby. The witnesses are,—

Philip, abbot of Lavingden, Bucks,
Master Robert Corcie,
John Blundell,
William de Cadindone,
Clerks and others.

The seals of two of these witnesses are represented by photographs in Dunstable town hall.

LIST OF THE PRIORS AND RECTORS OF DUNSTABLE.

The following list of the Roman and Protestant clergy of Dunstable has been compiled from the *Annales Priovatus de Dunstaplia*, from the Lincoln Registers, from the list in the Public Record Office, from the Church Register, from Dugdale's *Monasticon*, and from many other sources. There is no complete record extant; each list is more or less imperfect. Great help has been given to me with the list of rectors by Frederick A. Page-Turner, Esq., Brighton, and William Page, Esq., of St. Albans, has given me assistance with the priors. A copy of the list was sent by me to the registrar of Lincoln, asking for its collation with the records kept at Lincoln; but the reply given was, "There is not in existence a list wherewith I could collate yours." The MS. lists, both ancient and modern, vary in the spelling of the names. The scribes appear to have taken no pains beyond an attempt to represent the local pronunciation as nearly as letters would give it. For instance, in the *Annales*, one prior is named Wederhous, Wederhore, Wederhose, Wederour, Waderhyr, Wederov, and Wederow; and William de Breton is de Barton, de Brothan. The dates vary slightly Dates and names from printed books cannot be implicitly relied upon, however excellent the books may be. Printers' errors are as numerous as scribes' errors.

As far as I am aware, no list has hitherto been printed of the priors and rectors of Dunstable from the twelfth century to the present time.

PRIORS.

Bernard.
Cuthbert.
Thomas, occurs 1185, resigned 1202.
Richard de Morins, elected 1202, died 1242.
Geoffrey of Barton, elected 1242, resigned 1262.
Simon of Eaton, elected 1262, died 1274.
William le Breton, elected 1274, deposed 1280.
William de Wederhore, elected 1280, resigned 1302.
John of London, elected 1341, resigned 1348.
Roger of Gravenhurst, elected 1348, resigned 1351.
Thomas Marshall, elected 1351, resigned 1413.

H

John Roxton, elected 1413, resigned 1473.
Thomas Gylys, elected 1473, resigned 1482.
Richard Charnock, elected 1482, resigned 1500.
John Wastell, elected 1500, died 1525.
Gervase Markham, elected 1525, surrendered 1540.

PROTESTANT CLERGY.

1458, June 18, Robert Russell.
1554, Nov. 13, John Cooper.
15 . .   Collier, min., bur. 12 May, 1558.
1558,   William Walker, clk., bur. 18 Mar., 1584.
1588, Jan. 14, Joh'es Barns, D.D.
               John Richardson, B A., mar. 1605.
1609,   Edward Alport. min.
1625,   Zachary Symes.
1634,   Wm. Pedder.
1659,   Isaac Bringhurst and rector of Toddington.
1661, Feb. 21, Bp. Lyster, clk., lic. curate.
1662, April 2, Bp. Lyster, A.B., inst. rector, also vicar of
               Kensworth.
166 .,   Willm. Wimpew, preb. of Lincoln.
1671,   Willm. Jackson.
1681, May 10, Wm. Bedford, M.A.
1683, Feb. 11, John Lord, M.A., also vicar of Kensworth.
1728, Apr. 26, Thomas Hill, A.B.
1754, Jan. 2, John Lockman, M.A.
1769, Dec. 7, Samuel Judd Collins.
1800, Feb. 20, Wm. Mead.
1824. June 25, Solomon Piggott.
1845, June 12, Frederick Hose, M.A.
1884, Oct. 12, John Heyrick Macaulay, M.A.
1903, July 22, William Wing Carew Baker, M.A.

The original M.S. of the *Dunstable Annales* is in the British Museum. It is written in double columns, on parchment. It is available in a printed form, in Latin, amongst the *Annales Monastici*, published, under the direction of the Master of the Rolls, by Messrs. Longmans & Co., 1866. Hearn's edition of the *Annales*, printed in 1733, is a copy from a transcript made by Humphrey Wanley, and not from the original. The events from 1202 to the end of the year 1241 were compiled by Richard de Morins, prior of Dunstable from 1202 to 1242. The entries prior to 1201 are copies from the *Abbreviationes Chronicorum* and the *Imagines Historiarum* of Radulphus de Diceto, with a few extracts from Martinus Polonus, Florence of Worcester,

The "Annales Prioratus de Dunstaplia."

and others.   The *Annales* stop at 1297, but various entries have been made by different hands to 1459.   The work is not only a history of Dunstable in the thirteenth century, with the doings of the priors and townsfolk, but in part a history of England and of Europe of that period, as seen from the Dunstable standpoint.

The accompanying illustration is a photographic reproduction, the size of the original, of five lines from the *Annales* :—

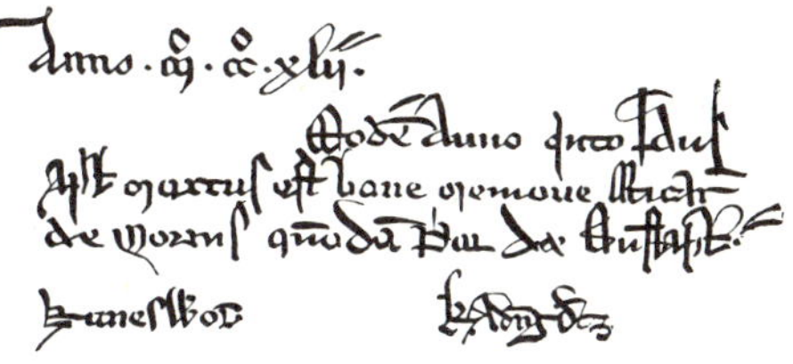

Fig. 14.   SENTENCE FROM THE *Annales Prioratus de Dunstaplia*.
SIZE OF ORIGINAL.

As written in abbreviated Latin, the words read :—

> Anno . m. cc. xlii.
>   Eode anno qnto Idus
>   Apis mortus est bon memorie Rich
>   de Morins quoda Pri de Dunstapl

> Kuneswor   Kadngdon

Kensworth and Caddington are added to the illustration from another part of the page to show the old mode of writing and spelling these names.   With the omitted letters supplied the entry reads :—

> Anno . m. cc. xlii.
>   Eodem anno, quinto, Idus
>   Aprilis, mortuus est bonæ memoriæ Richardus
>   de Morins, quondam Prior de Dunstaple.

> Kunesworth   Kadingdon.

The translation is :—

Year MCCXLII.
     In the same year (*i.e.* 1242) on the fifth day before
   the Ides of April, Richard de Morins, of excellent memory,
   (and) at one time Prior of Dunstable, died.
        Kensworth,   Caddington.

The 13th of April represents the Ides of April of old times; the prior, therefore, died on the fifth day before the 13th, viz., on the 8th of April, old style, 18th new style.

The seal of Dunstable is clearly described in heraldic terms in the *Notitia Monastica* as follows:—

The Seal of the Town and Priory. S. a pile in point A, a horseshoe conjoined, or, and interlaced with an annulet of the second pendant.

The meaning of this is that the ground of the shield is black, with a white or silver pile depending from the upper part. Conjoined to the pile is a horseshoe of gold, and interlaced with the horeshoe is a large golden ring.

Fig. 15. ARMS OF DUNSTABLE.

Arms of towns usually refer—often in a punning fashion, to some characteristic of the towns themselves, and Dunstable is no exception to the rule. Every word and symbol of the Dunstable arms has a distinct meaning.

The black ground refers to the first syllable of the word Dunstable, as "dun." Dun not only means a hill, but a colour, "dun" being almost equivalent with "black." Lady Macbeth, in summoning deep darkness to cover the murder of Duncan, says—Act i. sc. 5,—

Come, thick night,
And pall thee in the dunnest smoke of hell.

The pile refers to the second syllable "staple." "Staple," or "stapel," meant a market, because the old market-places were staked out with piles or pointed stakes called "stapels." The pile on the Dunstable arms represents a point of one of the wooden stakes of the Market-place in the time of Henry I.

Prior to the time of the first Henry, Dunstable experienced very bad luck in the way of fire, sword, and robbery. The king was most desirous that good luck should succeed bad. Horseshoes were believed to bring good luck, so a horseshoe of gold was selected as an emblem for the middle of the shield. In old times the horseshoe, when used for good luck, was invariably represented with the ends upwards, like a cup, as shown in the illustration, because in this position it would *hold the luck*, in the same way as old folks still say that a moon on its back "holds the rain," and a moon on its side is a "dripping moon," If the horseshoe had been represented arms downwards, or sideways, all the luck would have run out. The horseshoe, then was a golden cup full of good luck for Dunstable.

The last emblem is the *annulet*, or large ring of gold, pendant from the horseshoe. This had only one meaning in the time of Henry I., viz., nobility and jurisdiction. It was a gage and emblem of royal favour and protection.

The meaning of the arms, then, is that King Henry I., by his royal favour gave a golden cup full of good luck to the market town of Dunstable.

The modern arms of Dunstable, as represented on the borough seal, and on and in the Town Hall, copied from a stone carving of late date, are absolutely meaningless. The central object is not the heraldic pile, and the great golden horseshoe has become an insignificant loop of iron, driven into a small piece of wood. As ill-fortune will have it, this loop is represented *on its side*, in which position all good luck invariably runs away and gets wasted. Believers in emblems will say that good luck will never be restored to Dunstable till the founder's royal gift of the golden horseshoe is presented in a proper manner.

Amongst thirteenth century antiquities of the highest **The Eleanor Cross.** class, Dunstable is certainly very much poorer to-day from the total loss of the "lofty cross"—so called by Prior William de Wederow—which once stood in the market-place in honour of Eleanor, the wife of Edward I.

The queen died at Hardby, five miles west of Lincoln, on November 28th, 1290, and the funeral procession started from Lincoln for London on December 4th. It was arranged by the king and his friends that the body of the queen should stop at the chief religious houses on the way; this made the journey a somewhat circuitous one, as it was necessary that the body should be taken through Woburn, Dunstable, St. Albans, and Waltham. The body of the queen rested for one night at Dunstable; the bier stopped on the market-place, as it was pre-arranged that the body of the queen should rest on the precise spot on which the cross should be afterwards erected. At night the coffin was removed from the bier, taken into the now demolished choir of the church, and placed before the high altar. During the stay at Dunstable prior Wederow superintended the staking out of the ground for the cross, and sprinkled holy water over the earth. Dunstable and St. Albans are the only two places of which any contemporary written record is extant of the religious solemnities observed during the journey from Lincoln to Westminster. A gift was made to Dunstable, so the *Annales* informs us, of two precious cloths and about 120 lbs. of wax.

The cross at Dunstable was mainly erected by John Bello, or John de Bello, who had also the crosses of Northampton, Stony Stratford, Woburn, and St. Albans under his supervision. The figure of the queen and the other fine figures with which the Dunstable and other crosses were enriched were the work of William Torel, the London goldsmith, the designer of the life-size figure of Henry III., a full-size photograph of which is in the town hall, Dunstable.

Not a fragment of the Dunstable cross now appears aboveground. It stood on the west side of the High Street, opposite the " Red Lion " hotel, near the place now ornamented by a horse-trough. It was close to a house, now destroyed, which faced London, called Cross House. The cross is said to have been demolished by soldiers under the Earl of Essex in 1643. During alterations to the roadway in recent times parts of the foundation have been met with.

CHAPTER X.

———

Cromwellian and Coaching Times at Dunstable.

IN the later troublous times of Charles I. Bedfordshire
was almost wholly Cromwellian.   Lord Clarendon
says the king " had not any visible party in this county."
The party of Bedfordshire was that of
the " eastern associates," under the Earl
of Manchester.   Under this leader
Cromwell commanded the horse.   In October, 1643,
Prince Rupert was sent by the king with 2,000 to
3,000 horse besides foot soldiers into Bedfordshire,
then strongly occupied by the associates. Prince Rupert,
or Sir Lewis Dyve, first appeared at Ampthill, and then
went on to Bedford, where he took a number of Parliamentary officers prisoners.   On his departure, Colonel
Montague, of the Parliamentary party, got into Bedford
by a trick, and took off money and horses intended for
the king.   The king himself passed twice through the
county.

During the Commonwealth.

Coins of Charles I. are now and again picked up at
Dunstable. I have a disc of silver found at Dunstable
the size of a half-crown most beautifully engraved on
both sides by Simon de Passe. It is in perfect condition.
On one side is a most artistic and highly finished portrait
of Charles I.; on the other, the head of his queen,
Henriette Maria.

The first stage coach passed through Dunstable on Monday, April 12th, 1742. It started from the "Rose" inn, Holborn, on Monday afternoon and reached Litchfield through Birmingham on the Wednesday afternoon following. It returned on Thursday morning and arrived in London on Saturday night. On the return journey in the winter the coach arrived in Dunstable from the north after dark, as it passed slowly through the town it was escorted by men carrying lanterns. The utmost speed allowed, even for mails, was six and a-half miles per hour. The country between Dunstable and Hockliffe was then infested with thieves.

Chalk Hill, to the north of Dunstable, presented great difficulties for coaches, seven or eight horses were required to take the coach from Brewer's Hill Road to the top of the hill. The present cutting had not then been made, and the road over the hill was the ancient Roman road in a straight line over the hill-top from Dunstable to Hockliffe. The coaches were taken over the hill for forty years. In 1782 a new road was made in an attempt to obviate the ascent of the hill. This road branched to the left at Brewer's Hill Road, skirted the bottom of hill which it left on the right, and emerged at the bottom of the valley near where Mr. Scrogg's farmhouse now stands; it then skirted the east side of the present Hockliffe Road to Gibbet Arch and afterwards passed a little to the right of the present road before Tilsworth turning is reached, as shown on the map. The purchase of land and completion of this serpentine road cost £16,000. The money might have been better expended in excavating the straight Roman road over the hill.

At the height of the coaching period eighty stage coaches passed through Dunstable every day. Dunstable was then reached from London in about three hours fifty minutes allowing for a short stay, for breakfast, at Redbourn. The coach time tables were timed to minutes, as railway time tables are now. The "Wonder" coach, which started from the "Bull and Mouth" Hotel, London, at 6.30 a.m., was due at Dunstable at 10.21 a.m. Sometimes a stoppage was made for twenty minutes at Dunstable for dinner. The following is a "Sugar Loaf" hotel menu :—

Boiled round of beef.
Roast loin of pork.
Roast Aitchbone of beef.
Boiled hand of pork with peas pudding and parsnips.
Roast goose.
Boiled leg of mutton.

Two years before the London and Birmingham railway was opened for traffic, viz., in 1836, the number of coaches had become reduced to thirty-two daily, in 1837 the number was twenty-eight, and in the beginning of 1838, on the opening of the railway, only twelve coaches passed daily through the town, and in the latter part of 1838 coaching times were practically over.

At this time posting had been reduced to one half its former condition, and the number of cattle and sheep brought to the market of Dunstable had been reduced to the same extent.

The posting declined at the "Sugar Loaf" Hotel from £2,492 in 1837-8, to £1,005 in 1838-9.

The House accommodation from £3,191 in 1837-8 to £1,297 in 1838-9.

One year before the coaches had ceased to run, viz.: in 1837, the commissioners thought that if a cutting were made through the Chalk Hill and the serpentine road abandoned, that coaches might return and compete with the new railway, so the lowering of the road was executed in that year at a cost of £10,000. The coaches, however never returned.

When coaching times were at their busiest, resur-
Resurrectionists. rectionists, or "body-snatchers," were active in the neighbourhood of Dunstable. The Dunstable district was the northern limit from London. A certain family, whose descendants still live in the town, got a good living at this peculiar calling. Village burials were watched for, and the night after the funeral the body was sometimes taken from the grave and driven to London, where a ready sale was found amongst doctors. The bodies were usually taken amongst bundles of straw, but boxes and sacks of all

sorts were utilised.   A relative of my own was disinterred at Kensworth.   A husband buried his wife on a
Saturday.   Early on the Sunday morning, before folks
were about, the husband went to his wife's grave.   The
body, in grave-clothes, lay in the churchyard by the side
of the grave.   The resurrectionists had probably been
seriously frightened, and went off without the body.   A
hole had been dug at the head of the grave, the head of
the coffin broken away, and the body drawn out with a
hook caught under the chin.   The hole at the head of
the grave was small, and if it had been carefully filled in,
no one—so I was told—would have suspected that the
grave had been rifled.

Photograph]   [A. W. Smith.
Henry III.   Benefactor of Dunstable.
From the Bronze Effigy in Westminster Abbey

CHAPTER XI.

———

Pleasant Walks near Dunstable.

The footpaths and tracks referred to in this chapter are clearly shown in the map drawn by the Author.

DUNSTABLE is justly famous for its beautiful, grassy hills, or downs, three in number—(1) **The Hills.** Dunstable Downs, on the south-west; (2) Totternhoe Hill, on the west; and (3) Blows Downs, on the east. The hills range in height from 525 feet to 800 feet above the sea-level.

To reach Totternhoe Hill, West Street must be traversed to the " Rifle Volunteer " inn at its western termination—three-quarters of a-mile. The cemetery is passed on the left. On reaching the " Rifle Volunteer " the Icknield Way will be seen to continue on the border of the downs for a long distance on the left. Two other roads start from this point, the one to the left leads to Kensworth and Whipsnade, the one to the right, is the Green Way or Drover's Way, which leads to the top of Totternhoe Hill. If, instead of turning at once to the right, a few steps are taken along the Icknield Way a second road to the right will be seen, this leads to the ancient village of Totternhoe.

Before we start on a walk to Totternhoe Hill we should remember that the crossing of the roads near the " Rifle Volunteer " is one of the most ancient crossings of any great roads of England. The Icknield Way is an ancient British road of high antiquity, and the Green Way or Drover's Way is another of the same age, and the precursor of the Roman road which passes north and south, through Dunstable. Owing to comparatively modern alterations, the ancient crossing was not exactly where it now is, but about 300 feet nearer the cemetery than the " Rifle Volunteer " inn, about one-third of the distance to the cemetery from the inn. *See cross on Map.*

We are at the end of West Street with the Green Way, Drover's Way, or ancient British road to the right ; as we turn into this old way we see a group of whiting sheds on the left ; on old maps the site of these sheds is named Cold Harbour—*see page* 57 ; on other maps the place is named Pest House, in reference to the former presence of two very old cottages which were, in times of cholera long ago, used as make-shift isolation hospitals. The ground on which the sheds now stand is Pest House Close, and the field-way which passes at an angle through it, in the direction of Totternhoe, is Pest House path.

As we start on our breezy walk we note a long plantation of fir and beech trees on our right. These trees in all seasons shelter pedestrians from the east and north-east winds. On the left an extensive and beautiful valley gradually opens into view.

In the summer, wild plants of considerable interest may be seen in the plantation, including one of the rarer orchids; whilst the fields on the left produce wild plants of still greater interest, especially the rarer poppies.

The first 800 feet of the Green Way is comparatively modern, the next one-and-a-half miles is on the site of the ancient British trackway itself. A quarter of a mile from the West Street corner we reach a stile, amongst trees, on the right; this starts a pleasant field-way back to Dunstable. As we proceed, the vale on the left becomes more extensive and beautiful. At less than half a mile from West Street, the Green Way is crossed by the Brewers'-Hill Road; the turn to the left leads to Totternhoe, the one to the right by road and field to Dunstable—the field-path is on the right soon after the farm buildings are passed. A few years ago a long and costly law-suit decided that the road, from A to B on Map, was public; it had been gated at both ends and held as private for many years. Soon after we pass the Brewers' Hill crossing, the old-world village of Totternhoe may be seen embowered and partly hidden by trees. Beyond Totternhoe, the beautiful church of Edlesborough is seen, built upon a very large natural knoll, or small hill of hard chalk. Beyond Edlesborough, a little to the left, is Ivinghoe Hill, or Ivinghoe Beacon. The wood-covered hills continued on to the left are the Chiltern Hills; those in the far distance are White Hill and Haddington Hill, beyond Tring, in Buckingham-shire. Further on in the Green Way the road is crossed by a grassy road, named the Houghton Green Way; the turn to the left leads to Totternhoe, that on the right by green-way to Sewell and by footh-paths to Dunstable Chalk Hill and Houghton Regis. If we, for a moment, here take the way to the right for a short distance, and then abruptly turn again to the left by another Green-Way, we reach, on the left, the wonderful and perhaps unique, ancient British Camp named Maiden Bower (see *Maiden Bower*. p. 38). We return to the old Green Way, and proceed. A grassy excavation which is soon reached, on the left, is " Rag Pit," or " Jack King's Pit," named after a man who, many years ago, was here crushed by a fall of chalk. We now come to another green crossing. This is Sewell Way; the Green Way on the left is a footway only, and leads to Totternhoe through the recreation ground. The way on the right is a foot-way only to Sewell although farmers use it as a road way; there is, however, no Green Way for vehicles. Farmer's carts are driven over a dangerous tramway from the large chalk-pits close by into the Sewell Way.

After passing the Sewell Way, six small embankments will be passed on the right-hand of, and at right angles to, the main Way; just after the sixth bank is passed there is a footpath to the right, which leads to the north base of the hill by Wheelbarrow Way, Cow Lane, and across the railway by a level-crossing on to Cow Common and the Litany—a hunting-ground greatly esteemed by zoologists and botanists. On looking down this path, ancient linces will be seen on the sloping hill-side on the left.

Still proceeding towards Castle Hill, the road is soon crossed by still another Green Way, named Wheel-barrow Way—a corruption of Wilbury Way—to the right and Quarry Way to the left. At this point there is an easily overlooked footpath running diagonally from the first corner of the cross Ways to the right; this path leads over the undulating hills seen in front, towards the lime kilns and to Sewell and Dunstable.

Wheelbarrow Way leads to the Litany, and by a road to the left, just before reaching Cow Lane, over a tram-way to Stanbridge Ford railway-station. Quarry Way leads to Church End, Totternhoe. From this point we see half-buried in trees in the distance on the right, beyond the railway, the villages of Stanbridge and Tilsworth. Beyond these villages different hills and beau-tiful undulating country is seen as far as the eye can reach. When the air is clear and the light favour-able, the grand spire of Leighton Buzzard Church may be seen. Close to Wheelbarrow Way four ancient linces, or terraces, on the hill-side come in view on the right. These linces, or terraces, cultivated on the flat surface, are not modern works ; they were made in Saxon and mediæval times, when the farmers of old toiled on the hill sides with a clumsy plough of wood drawn through the hard soil by sometimes as many as eight or ten oxen, two or more abreast. Between the railway and the villages are the old bush-covered pasture called *Cow Common*, and the *Litany*, the latter so named after certain religious services connected with the "beating of the bounds," in mediæval times. At or near this *Quarry Way* crossing, the main trackway of the ancient British road is lost. The old road left Totternhoe Knoll on the left and proceeded through Stanbridge, Eggington, and Great Brickhill to Fenny Stratford. At its junction with the latter place, the Romans re-made it as part of their great military road to Chester. Every foot of the ground, however, on which we now stand at Totternhoe Hill is rich in ancient British associations, and we proceed to the last green crossing, called Combe Way ; the way to the left leads to Middle-End and Totternhoe Church, the one to the right, to Lower End, Totternhoe. We may here turn for a moment, and note Dunstable Downs, with the five tumuli, and the great plateau on the hill-top to the right. A few steps further to the west we reach a fence and gate. On the left is a most beautiful valley, with linces near the top of the steep hill. Beeches and other trees grow from near the top to the bottom of the slope. The valley can be descended by the linces from this point, if desired.

Visitors in carriages cannot proceed further than the fence, and if it is proposed to spend a considerable time on this magnificent hill-top, the carriages should be taken down Combe Way to the village, and left at one of the inns. It would not be safe to take any horse or vehicle through the fence on to the hill, as a grassy precipice is on the left side. The "Cross Keys" inn and "Jordan's," in Chapel Lane are favourite resorts, where horses can be put up and good homely accommodation secured.

Photograph]   Middle End Totternhoe.   A. Strange.

Totternhoe is only a small old-world village with limited powers for catering.

On passing through the gate a row of beech trees is seen on the right, these grow in a well preserved Roman ditch. The flat field beyond the ditch is the area of a small Roman Camp, with a second dry Roman ditch on the right and a precipice on the left. Totternhoe Knoll or Castle Hill, is situated to the west on the other side of a third Brito-Roman ditch. The huge Knoll is an ancient British look-out position and fire-beacon, and the depression made for the rude furnace on the top is clearly visible. The large hollow on the east side of the Knoll is popularly called the " Money Pit." The earthworks on this part of the hill are ancient British, and older than Roman.

The hill is 524 feet above the level of the sea, and 170 feet above the valley to the south. The steep hill may be descended to the village below by more than one footpath. On the north there is a field-way by Cow Lane and across the railway to the Litany, Stanbridge, and Tilsworth.

A long spring, summer or autumn day may be most enjoyably spent on this hill. In all seasons alike it is delightful. In summer the Green Way is carpeted with flowers. Campanulas, Hawkweeds, Potentillas, and Scabious are the prevailing common plants. The soft elastic turf is fragrant with Wild Thyme. The invigorating, health-giving air is alive with larks,—nightingales swarm at the foot of the hill. Butterflies peculiar to chalk districts occur, and uncommon birds and insects are frequently seen. The whole place, with the Litany below, is in a state of wild nature. The prevailing trees are beech, and in autumn, when the leaves, still upon the trees, have changed in colour to gold and bronze, the sight of the valley as seen from the hill-top is one never to be forgotten. In wintry and stormy weather the hill is generally deserted, few persons can stand against the force of a south-western gale on this hill. The villagers below are entirely protected from the cold winds.

The earthworks are described fully in pp. 38-41.

For Totternhoe Church, *see page* 137.

The end of West Street must be reached as before, and the Pest-house foot-path taken into **Alternative Ways to Totternhoe Hill.** the Dunstable Way to Totternhoe, or the Green Way may be traversed as far as Houghton Way, or even Sewell foot-way, both on the left. The last way is the more grassy, pleasant, and wild; it begins as a Green Way, but is a footway only, and ends as a foot-path branching to the left, which passes diagonally through the Recreation Ground. The hill on the right is Coxen Hill. When Totternhoe is reached, a return to Dunstable can be made, if desired, by Houghton Way, Brewers' Hill Way, or Lancott Hill. To reach Totternhoe Hill after leaving the Recreation Ground, a turn must be made abruptly to the right; the road leads to the base of the hill. A very pleasant way is by Crab-tree Path, across Quarry Way into Combe Way, as shown on the map. On reaching Combe Way, one has almost reached the top of the hill, and a deep wooded valley, partly cut into linces, is seen on the left. A descent can be made over these linces if desired, or the linces can be followed in various directions. If Combe Way is followed, it takes the visitor entirely round the hill.

The hill may also be reached by continuing in the road from the Recreation Ground past the School and and Combe Way, both on the right, till the "Cross Keys" inn is nearly reached. Here a white gate will be seen on the right; the path from here branches both to the right and left, and the hill may be ascended by an ancient Way amongst trees in either direction. This part of the hill is most beautiful and romantic, and a considerable time may be enjoyably spent on the ancient trackway at the base and on the grassy linces above. If the visit is made on a hot summer's day, agreeable shade will be found amongst the trees on the hill-side. A similar descent in winter enables the visitor to escape from the cold north and north-east winds.

Another route is to proceed along West Street to Victoria Street, walk to the end and cross over Chiltern Road to the swing gate, then follow the long field-path, crossing Brewer's Hill Road. Cross the road and proceed through two other fields and cross the New Sewell Way, leaving Maiden Bower on the left as shown on the map, a corner can be cut off the New Sewell Way by the field-path if desired, then go by road under the tramway bridge on the left— the road to the right leads into the village of Sewell. Keep to the road, do not ascend the banks into the fields on the left. Keep the lime kilns on the right. Immediately after leaving the kilns there is a footpath on the left almost opposite, and a blind farmer's road, which latter passes under the railway, on the right. If the footpath is followed it will lead to the junction of Wheelbarrow Way with the Green Way to Totternhoe Hill, not far from the hill itself.

The fieldpath just described from Chiltern Road to the New Sewell Way is almost on the site of an ancient trackway from the British Camp named Wanlud's Bank, near Leagrave, to the chief entrance of Maiden Bower. Large numbers of ancient stone implements have been found near this trackway in its course of more than four miles. The path over the grassy hills to the Totternhoe Hill Green Way is romantically beautiful and perfectly wild. Uncommon wild plants and sometimes certain of the rarer orchids may be gathered on these hills at the proper seasons. Near by, both near Maiden Bower and by Wheelbarrow Way are large accumulations of chalk-waste, this dry, crumbly, small material forms a suitable place of growth for a series of interesting wild plants.

It will take some time to explore the steep grassy slopes between the lime kilns and the Green Way. In one valley will be seen at the extreme bottom the ruined entrances to the long quarry passages from which Totternhoe stone was extracted in mediæval times for the building of local churches and mansions. The great church and priory of Dunstable, as well as parts of St. Albans Cathedral and Westminster Abbey were built of this stone. The hills at this place are said to be honey-combed with galleries made in past times in the search for this material. That the passages extend for long distances is certain, as the writer, aided by cords, and a lantern has traversed some of them. The subterranean passages, are wet and unsafe, as the chalk has fallen in from above, and has made exploration difficult and, in some of the passages, impossible.   The stone is exposed on the surface in certain places, and was known to the ancient Britons and Romans as well as the mediæval builders.

A path from the north by Banbury Knap, which crosses the tramway to the junction of Wheelbarrow **Walks from Totternhoe Hill into the Valleys.** Way and Cow Lane, leads over the railway by a level crossing to the Litany and Cow Common.   This wild place is a paradise for field naturalists ; it is everywhere watered by sparkling, unpolluted watercourses : in some places it is bushy and in others open common.   It is seldom visited except by an occasional shepherd or farmer's man, so that animal and plant life exist there practically undisturbed.   The footpaths, as shown by the map, lead over rich pastures and tiny rivulets to Stanbridge, Tilsworth, Sewell, and Dunstable.   The three former old-world villages can be easily visited, if time permits.   The fields are nearly all rich, damp pastures with the beautiful wild plants belonging to such positions ; the water-courses are full of aquatic plants and insects, with a few fish and some of the birds that love the water-side.

The hill can be descended from the south by the oblique path near the junction of the British with the Roman camp to Chapel Lane.   On entering Chapel Lane, " Jordan's," where refreshment is provided, is on the right.   Lower down a brook is crossed, and the path passes at an angle through a small plum orchard, where a wooden bridge has to be crossed and the path followed through two fields to Honey-wick Lane, or at the end of the first field two gates may be passed at a field-corner and a most beautiful pasture crossed at an angle, as shown on map.   The pastures here are of the richest class, and surrounded by large, well-grown trees.   If the state of the crops admits, a little divergence may be made near the starting-point of the angular path for a glance at the deep and dangerous Hulyam's Moat, shown on map.   Honey-wick Lane should be traversed from end to end : it is a place to linger in.   There are tall ivy-grown trees on one side, and a hedge and brooklet, with a few ancient cottages on the other.   The never-ceasing tinkling of the brook, the incessant song of the birds, including that of the nightingale, and the rich, flowery hedge-banks, make this place a delight.   No place could be better for lover's vows.   Honey-wick Lane leads by a brook-side field-path, and then across lovely flat fields, here and there with wooden bridges across pleasant water-courses to Totternhoe.   A return from Honey-wick to Totternhoe Hill may be made in the Totternhoe direction by the, at first, little angular footpath in West Field marked on map.   This leads across a large arable field, then across a damp field-corner with a pond full of plant and animal life—a model place of rest for members oɪ a Field Club—and then through a narrow, rich meadow into the Totternhoe Road, almost exactly opposite the white swing gate with the ancient green trackways beyond to the hill-top.   If cakes, ginger-beer, milk, ale, or bread-and-butter are wanted, there is the " Cross Keys " inn, almost opposite the white gate.

Dunstable Downs. Dunstable Downs are very accessible from Dunstable and can be traversed for more than two miles.   At the highest part near the turning to Whipsnade they are 800 feet above the level of the sea, and the view over the country to the west is only bounded by the horizon.   The downs are one long, almost treeless, stretch of short, elastic turf, fragrant with wild thyme and rich with the well-known flora belonging to chalk downs.   In the more crumbly chalk, usually at the base of the hills, many orchids grow, including some of the rarer species.   The air on these hills is absolutely pure, there being no source of pollution from towns or factories.   The west wind sweeps almost unbroken from the Atlantic, and no one can wander over the downs without benefitting from the pure breeze.

West Street must be traversed to the end and the ascent of the hill made by the broad Green Way on the left, till the Five Knolls are reached.   This point was an ancient British look-out station which com-

Photograph]   **Dunstable Downs from the Icknield Way beyond Well-Head.**   [H. A. Strange.

manded the two great roads. From the first seat on the hill-top an obscure, grassy trackway dating from ancient British times, may be seen on the left which descends the hill and crosses the fields to Maiden Bower. The seat is close to the hollow of an ancient British look-out hut, and other hut-foundations may be seen close by. We soon reach Pascombe pit, a combe which derives its name either from some Easter celebration, now forgotten, or from the Passe-flower or Pasque-flower, which at one time was no doubt as common on this hill as it still is on Barton, and other local chalk hills. At the bottom of the pit there once existed a large Roman platform of earth. It has recently been destroyed for the erection of targets. The strange old trackways should be noticed on the east side of the hill-top, these date from remote times and have been super-seded by the present road. One of the old track-ways can be traced into the Totternhoe Green Way, others into the field behind the " Rifle Volunteer " Inn, into the site of the ancient British road marked on map. In walking southwards several combes are passed and· a descent can be made, if desired, to Well Head, the source of the river Ouzel, which joins the great Ouze and empties itself into the sea near King's Lynn, in Norfolk.

At about a mile south of the Knolls there are two roads, the one on the left leads to Kensworth, that on the right to Whipsnade Heath. Near the junction of these two roads a vase full of Roman coins was found in 1770. They were probably not all carried away as one was found close by last year. Near the same junction are the sites, marked on Map, of two round tumuli from which two contracted human skeletons have been dug out. The downs can be traversed for more than another mile from this junction of roads. At half the distance there is a narrow and most beautiful lane on the left, this leads to Whipsnade Green and Whipsnade Heath. If the downs are traversed for another half-mile the hill is crossed by a public road, if the road is taken it leads to a famous pond named Ouzley pond on the right. By bearing to the left, past Dell Farm, Whipsnade Green is reached.

Near the crossing of the path and road on the downs, but at the bottom, and almost opposite Valence End Farm, is a fine group of ancient British hut remains.

The last mile of the downs is scored up and down by old ways, some trackways for foot passengers, other cutways for vehicles, but all now grass grown and practically disused except by health and pleasure-seekers. Some are of very ancient origin, and were in use before the present roads were made. In the days of our grand-fathers and great grandfathers they were used by farmers and by travellers from village to village. Several track-ways emerge from the opening of the beautiful narrow lane to Whipsnade Green or Common. Some can be slightly traced across fields now under cultivation.

The exposed hill to the west, at the termination of the two miles' stroll from the Knolls, is Edlesborough Hill, the traditional site of the first Edlesborough Church. To the left of this hill is the romantic Bibsall Spring.

The return to Dunstable can be made by the foot of the hill, if the base is preferred to the top, or by the Icknield Way, a quarter of a mile beyond the base of the hill. If Whipsnade Heath is reached, a stay can be made on this beautiful gorse-grown waste, and the birds, plants, and insects noted. The road to the north from the heath leads to the top of the downs and Dunstable. Directly the heath is passed there is a most beautiful narrow, fern-grown lane to the left that leads past Houchingsend and Hill farms to Whipsnade Common. After Landpark Wood—the home of the green helle-bore—is passed, on the road that leads north, there is another beautiful flowery lane on the right; this leads to Kensworth. On reaching this road, turn to the left, and the road again leads to the top of the downs and Dunstable. A field-path on the right, near the junction, aslo leads to Dunstable.

If, instead of taking the north road to Dunstable from Whipsnade Heath, the path is taken at the south-west corner of the heath, this will lead to Kensworth Road, and a little to the right, on emerging, a lane will be seen named Church End Road, or Hollix (Holly) Lane. This lane leads to Kensworth Church, and from this point

Photograph]   **Near Kensworth. A Dunstable Lane.**   [H. A. Strange.

Dunstable can be reached by Kensworth Lane. Most of the distance can be covered by field-paths, starting from the churchyard, as marked on the map.

If one is at Kensworth Church, and wishes to traverse the ancient British road which remains now much as it was in ancient British times, the two fields must be crossed by the path at the north-east corner of the churchyard ; this path leads into Kensworth Lane. On reaching the lane, turn immediately to the left, by a farmer's cart-way, across one field—hedge on right—and then turn again a few yards to the left, and next to the right. This is the British road ; farmers call it Down-Dell-Lane. Proceed for half a mile, and a field-path to the right leads straight to Dunstable. The path to the left leads to a pond—" Mount Pleasant " on map. On the west of the pond, large numbers of Neolithic stone implements have been found. One can proceed further down the British road if desired, past a barn on the left, and past Downs' Farm. The path turns to the left near the farm-house, and then the top of the Downs can be again reached. If the path is kept to the right after passing Downs' Farm, it leads to Downs' Lane. This lane is generally in a bad state, and in wet weather very muddy There is also a path at the back of the cemetery, but always muddy in wet weather. All the chalky fields on the east side of the downs have produced Neolithic implements, such as stone axes, adzes, arrow-heads, etc.

No refreshments are procurable on this excursion beyond what can be obtained at small village inns, and these are far apart, and on the hill non-existent. It is advisable, therefore, to take refreshment from Dunstable.

These downs, named after a Mr. Blow, a farmer, are on the east of and close to the town. They are **Blow's Downs.** less extensive than Dunstable Downs; the height is 700 feet above the level of the sea. From Church Street railway-station they are reached by the footpath by Long Hedge, and from the south of the town, by the foot-path in Great Northern Road or by Half-Moon Lane.

The paths all lead to the western foot of the Downs, and the hills may be ascended from here at once, or the footpaths taken to right or left. If the ascent is made over ancient, grass-grown cartways, paths can be taken right and left from the top of the hill corresponding with the paths below. The angle at the top represents an ancient British look-out station, with bases of huts. This station commanded the Icknield Way below. If the path on the top is taken towards Luton, a flat grassy artificial platform will be passed, and then, just before the lime works are reached, and on the slope of the downs, a group of ancient British hut-foundations will be seen. From a destroyed hut on the other side of the gully a human skeleton was dug out in 1888. The deep, grassy gully, valley, or pass, leads to Zouche's Farm. Proceeding eastwards, Skimpot Farm is seen on the other side of the railway. The name is a corruption of St. Mary's Pottery. "Skim" and "Skimmery" are well-known corruptions of "St. Mary." The pottery was on the top of the hill on the west side of Zouche's Farm, and near Skimpot Wood, where extensive remains still exist.

Close to Skimpot Farm the footpath to Luton becomes a road; if desired, a turn can be made to the left, under the railway-bridge, and Dunstable reached by the Icknield way. The road parallel with the railway leads straight to Luton; at half a mile along the road, at Chalk Farm, there is a sharp turning to the right, which leads to Caddington. The Luton road at this point becomes a beautiful footpath parallel with and near the railway; it first passes through a pasture, then through a gate into a field with woody linces on the right, and so on to Luton.

If the Caddington Road is taken at Chalk Farm, it leads up a pleasant but steep hill—Hill Lane—to Chaul End, then by a very pleasant lane straight to Caddington, passing on the way Hell Lane and Wicket Lane. When Chaul End is reached, and at the point where the road abruptly turns to the right, there is a footpath through a farmyard and by a pond on the left to Luton. This footpath is most pleasant and beautiful, leading over fields and by plantations. A little further on the Caddington Road to the left is another footpath to

Luton, and then Wicket Lane on the left. Wicket Lane is perfectly wild, and seldom traversed; it leads to Oak Road and Leagrave.

We must now return to Skimpot Farm and the junction of roads and paths near the railway-bridge. Opposite to the bridge, on the south side, are two grassy trackways cut up the hill; they are rather steep, but always beautiful and wild; either can be taken, as both lead to a sequestered lane on the hill-top. The lane passes Stanner's Wood on the right, and then a path is reached which passes at an angle right across a large arable field to an oak-tree. A stile is crossed into an ancient pasture; turn to the left by a hedge till another hedge is reached at right angles; go through the gate into an old pasture. Straight on, on the left is Hell Lane, which leads to Caddington and Luton; but leave the lane and keep to the right close along the high hedge, and then over a stile, through several fields, to Caddington. Folly Wood is passed on the right, as the village is neared. This path over the hill by lanes, fields, and old pastures, is seldom used, and should be much better known. It is a very ancient right of way, named Church Way.

When at Caddington pass the church on the left and adjoining the churchyard on the east is a path back to Dunstable by the side of Badger-dell Wood and through Round Wood (which happens to be square) and by the side of the site of the late Daffy Wood to Runley Lane, after the site of Daffy Wood is passed, Dunstable is reached by the road and path on the left. Like the last, this beautiful, and in some places, romantic path is seldom used. Badger-dell Wood points to the presence of badgers in times past. Countrymen for sport would sometimes put badgers under wheelbarrows and bate them with dogs. To " bite like a badger " is still a local proverbial phrase.

We now return to the base of Blows Downs, near Dunstable, where the paths and cut-ways run to the south. Either the top or bottom of the hill can be taken. The tracks lead to Caddington. The top of Blows Downs which overlooks the high road was the site of the " priors gallows" in the thirteenth century. The name of the site is given as "Edesuthe," which from the accompanying contemporary description of the position is equivalent with East Street, or the Street fields on the east side of the Roman road. The site was probably on the upper flat lince, near the hedge which divides at right angles the Downs from the adjoining arable field.

The path to Caddington passes through the top of the arable field to Dame Ellen's Wood, past Little John's Wood into Caddington Lane and Caddington. As soon as Dame Ellen's Wood is passed there is a field path on the left with a hedge to the right. This also leads to Caddington, past Castle-croft Wood and then over a stile or through a hedge gap to the right. The path then obliquely crosses a large arable field. A large grassy or pasture-like corner is next cut off to a hedge. The hedge can be followed keeping it on the left, but there is a deep and romantic hollow lane beneath the hedge—Gully Lane— which can be descended and followed. In certain seasons this is a perfect fairy glen, completely covered with the branches of trees from the high banks on both sides*, the banks are loamy-clay, and in the proper seasons clad with various wild plants. This lane is more than half a-mile long, if the walk is continued to Caddington Lane, half way along there is a turn to the right to Bury Farm, opposite the turn, there is a footway that passes in an angular direction across arable fields to Caddington.

In returning from Caddington there are the fieldways previously described, but a change can be made by returning by Caddington Lane—the lane to Dunstable— east of the village. At a little more than a quarter of a-mile from Caddington a road crosses the lane right and left. The one on the left leads past an ancient building named Piper's Farm, the one on the right leads past Bury Farm, partly close to the farmyard and round the back of the farm, into Bury Farm Lane and Caddington Lane. It is a public carriage-way, but two large gates must be opened by tourists, if carriages are used. If the lane to Bury Farm is not taken, the lane, after proceeding for three-quarters of a-mile from Caddington,

---

*Since these notes were written the branches have been cut away, and many of the trees cut down.

comes to a sharp turn to the right. Just before the turn is reached a tumulus on the right is passed, in fact the ancient road has been cut through the south side of the mound as the fringe of the tumulus is in the opposite field. In taking the turn to the right, Bury Farm Lane is passed on the right at about half-a-mile. At the next gate on the left there is a fieldpath into the High Road ; this can be taken, or, if preferred, Caddington Lane can be traversed to its junction with the High Road or Roman Road to Dunstable. Caddington Lane is a very old trackway as is shown by its irregular, sinuous course, and by its varying width. It is a very pretty way, with hollies, wild cherries, and spindle trees on the hill. It is prolific in wild plants, and in autumn rich with the higher fungi. *Boletus rubinus*, a fine large terrestical fungus with blood-red pores was first met with in this lane and for many years this lane was the only known European locality. The upper part of the lane to Caddington and Slip End beyond, is famous as being the extensive site of the dwelling-places of Primeval men, they lived here in vast hordes by the sides of what were then large pools and swamps. The remains are found at a depth of from four to more than thirty feet beneath the present surface.

There are many other pleasant field-walks from Dunstable. Two on the east start by the paths south of Church Street railway-station. One leads to the ancient village of Houghton Regis, the other to the still more ancient villages of Leagrave and Limbury.

Another pleasant walk is at Kensworth Lane, south of the town. This can be traversed to Kensworth. After Pitchering Pond is passed on the left, two lanes branch from the left and one to the right ; the latter leads to the church ; either of the lanes to the left can be taken. Both are alike beautiful, and they converge near Kensworth Lynch by the high road to Dunstable. The lower is the ancient British road. The higher passes the old vicarage to Studham. Near the point of convergence in the fields to the south, a very large Common once existed named Kensworth Common ; it is now arable fields, partly used as brickfields. In the excavations for brick-earth, large quantities of Roman urns have been found, mostly broken, with mill-stones, hones, tiles, spindle-whorls, bones, etc., of Roman age.

To the north of Dunstable, as soon as the chalk-hill cutting is passed, there are field-paths on the right to Houghton Regis and Bidwell; and further on on the left there are field-ways to the old-world villages of Tilsworth and Stanbridge.

Houghton Regis Church.

CHAPTER XII.

Villages within easy reach of Dunstable.

WITHIN TWO MILES.

THE church, dedicated to All Saints, is chiefly decorated in style, it contains a fine Norman font, a canopied altar tomb to a knight, with the arms of Sewell, and two small brasses of priests. To the north of the village is Bidwell, the site of a former holy well, dedicated to St. Brigid; to the north-west is Thorn, a reputed site of Bunyan's preaching. A Bunyan chair is preserved in Houghton Regis Baptist Church. Houghton Hall, to the south, is the seat of the Brandreth family.

Houghton Regis.

The church, dedicated to St. Mary, has an early Norman north side, west end and door (now within the church) south doorway, and chancel arch. The two Norman doorways are remarkable, the capitals of the south door are carved with illustrations from

Kensworth.

the fables of Babrius, the Wolf and Heron and Eagle and Hare. Babrius is assumed to have been a Greek not later than A.D. 207, and not a Roman. The following are translations from the extant Latin.

The Wolf and Heron. A bone got firmly fixed in a wolf's throat, so he agreed with a heron, to check his sufferings, to put its neck down his throat and draw out the bone. For this service he promised a due reward. The bone was extracted and the heron claimed the prize, but the wolf with grinning teeth and eyes, said, " Oh no, you have received quite prize enough in getting your head safely out of my jaws." *Moral.*—One gets well repaid, if in aiding the bad, no hurts come to oneself.

The Kite and Snake. A kite attacked a snake and bore it aloft, the captive snake turned and fatally bit the kite. As the bird was dying the snake said,—" What frenzy possessed you to injure me who did no hurt to you ? What you designed for me you have received yourself.

The Norman work is A.D. 1150. There are two very deep " Donkey-wells " at Kensworth.

The original church was a simple oblong structure with an apse, there are no aisles, the tower is perpendicular, and the south porch, not the south door, modern. There is a stone staircase, on the north side of the chancel arch, now closed, to a former Rood gallery.

Totternhoe. The church, dedicated to St. Giles, the patron saint of cripples, is Perpendicular. There is a brass in the chancel to a vicar, 1524, and a remarkable carved *rebus* on the name of Ashwell, a probable benefactor, on the eastern pillar of the north side. The work represents an ash tree and well. The church probably owes its dedication to the close proximity of the stone quarries, where accidents must have frequently occurred, and a patron saint of cripples useful.

WITHIN FOUR MILES.

Hockcliffe. The church is dedicated to St. Nicholas, and contains an altar tomb. The site and some remains of the building belonging to the Knights Hospitallers mentioned in the *Annales Dunstaplia* is at Bull Farm, on the left, before Hockliffe is reached from

K

Photograph] Kensworth Church. [H. A. Strange.

Dunstable. There is some fine wood carving at the "White Hart" inn. There are earthworks south of the church.

The church, dedicated to All Saints, is partly in the decorated style, but now little better than a ruin, it contains two altar tombs with effigies of Knights.

Chalgrave.

The church dedicated to St. John is a modern, and unusually ugly modern structure of brick in Markyate Cell Park. A more modern and less ugly chancel of stone was added in 1892. The mansion named Markyate Cell, in the Park, is built on the site of a twelfth-century priory; this nunnery was given at the Dissolution to George Ferrers. The present mansion is said to be haunted by the ghost of a "wicked Lady Ferrers," who is associated with three successive destructions of the building by fire. See *Folk Lore*. The poet Cowper attended school at Markyate, but the building is now demolished. Beechwood Park, to the south-east of Markyate, is the seat of the Sebright family.

Markyate.

The church, dedicated to St. Mary Magdalen, is almost entirely modern, and of brick. There are only a few fragments in stone of the original church left. The chief attractions of Whipsnade are its fine Common and Heath.

Whipsnade.

The Church is dedicated to St. Mary. Externally, the architecture is Decorated and Perpendicular; internally, there is fine thirteenth-century work. There is a remarkable font, made from a richly carved capital of a pier. The capitals of the columns of the nave are finely carved examples of thirteenth century work. The building has been greatly injured by so-called "restorations." The original opening to the chancel was small, with hagioscopes on both sides; the latter have been destroyed, the chancel arch made new and large, and the eastern columns rebuilt; the western have also been manipulated. A few fragments of ancient tiles are in the church, and slight traces of old painting may be seen. The remaining portion of Studham Common is near the village, south-east of the church.

Studham.

The church is dedicated to All Saints. There is a
Caddington. re-built Norman door, some Early English
work, two sixteenth century brasses, and a
font inscribed round the rim with a " Palindrome,"—
NIΨON ANONHM A MHMONA NOΨIN. The
inscription reads backwards and forwards alike, and its
meaning is, " Wash my sins, not my face only." The
church is said to be built over a much older foundation,
and has been injured by " restoration." The district
is rich in relics of Primeval man.

Photograph]   **Font, Studham.**   [*A. W. Smith.*

There are no churches at these villages, except a new one at the latter place, dedicated to the Holy Trinity. **Leagrave, Limbury, and Biscott.** The whole district is famous for its ancient British, Saxon, and Mediæval remains, including a fine moated farm named Moat House. A large number of ancient stone implements, ancient British coins, Roman vases, and human skeletons have been found. At Leagrave is the source of the Lea and the ancient British Camp of Wanlud's Bank.

The church is dedicated to St. Margaret. It is chiefly Perpendicular and Decorated in style, and **Sundon.** has a good Early English font. To the south-west is Chalton. The brickyards north of the Midland Railway are on the site of a Saxon Cemetery.

West.

The church is dedicated to All Saints ; it is in various styles of architecture, chiefly Perpendicular. **Tilsworth.** It has a canopied effigy of an ecclesiastic, a Norman-French inscribed slab to Adam de Tullesworth, and an ancient reconstructed font. The building is in a ruinous state. In the churchyard is a stone in memory of a girl who was murdered in Blackgrove Wood close by. See *Folk Lore and Superstition.* At the moated farm opposite the church there is an ancient gatehouse and columbarium. There are earthworks close to the church.

The church is dedicated to St. John the Baptist, and has been completely restored ; there is **Stanbridge.** inside the church an Early English font, and examples of seventeenth century woodwork. Outside, opposite the south door, there is a remarkable boulder inscribed, with a rude cross. This is probably one of the earliest Christian antiquities of the Dunstable district. It is situated on the south side of the church near the porch, and was dug up at Christmas, 1858, from the bottom of a five or six feet grave close to where it now is. In raising the boulder it became broken in two, the missing part is said to be " somewhere in the churchyard."

Carved Pulpit, Canopy and part of Screen, Edlesborough.

Eaton Bray. The church is dedicated to St. Mary, and contains very fine Early English work. The iron-work on the south door is similar in style with that at Leighton Buzzard and on Queen Eleanor's tomb in Westminster Abbey; the work is by the same hand, that of Thomas de Lightone (Leighton), about 1293-4.

Edlesborough. The Church is dedicated to St. Mary. The nave is of the Decorated and Perpendicular periods; there is Early English work on the sedilia, and an unusually good geometrical east window. There are misereres and a fine Perpendicular wooden pulpit with canopy and Rood-screen. The church is a very fine one, built upon a great natural mound of hard chalk, it has been restored, and new paintings added in the spaces between the Nave arches.

About Five Miles—North.

Toddington. The church is dedicated to St. George; the transepts are private property, and are dedicated to St. James and St. Paul. The building contains fine monuments of the Cheyneys, Peyvres, and Wentworths; and there is a three-storeyed parvise or priest's chamber. The grotesque figures carved on the exterior of the church are worthy of notice. On the east of the village is a large round look-out mound, named Conger Hill. The present Manor House is built in the neighbourhood of the site of the residence of Sir Paulinus Peyvre, steward to Henry III. British, Roman, and mediæval antiquities have been found close to and within the manor grounds.

Streatley. The church is dedicated to St. Margaret. It is of the Perpendicular period, but contains an Early English font.

Battlesden. There is a small church dedicated to St. Peter, in which there is an ancient font.

Harlington. The church is dedicated to St. Mary, and belongs to the Perpendicular period, with a late Decorated arcade and window. At Samsell, one mile to the north, John Bunyan was in 1660 arrested whilst preaching in a cottage. He was brought before Francis Wyngate, at Harlington House, and committed for the first time, to Bedford Gaol.

SOUTH.

Little Gaddesden. The church is dedicated to St. Peter and St. Paul. It contains monuments of the Stanley and Bridgwater families. In this parish, John de Gaddesden, the old time physician, was born.

Flamstead. The church, dedicated to St. Leonard, is built in the Decorated style, but there is Norman and Early English work within. It contains an altar tomb with rudely executed figures of a man and woman, about 1400 There is a parvise or priest's chamber and a rood gallery with an external staircase. It contains monuments of the Saunders and Sebright families. There are some quaint inscriptions carved on the nave piers, dated 1590-7.

EAST.

Stopsley. The church is dedicated to St. Thomas. It was built in 1861. Palæolithic implements and fossil bones have been found a little to the south at Round Green and Ramridge End.

WEST.

Eggington. A small church, dedicated to St. Michael, of the Early English and Decorated Periods.

Slapton. The church, dedicated to Holy Cross, is of the Late Decorated and Perpendicular Periods, there is a brass to James Tornay, yeoman at arms to Henry VIII., and his two wives and nine children, 1519, and a small effigy of a priest, 1462.

Ivinghoe. A cruciform church, dedicated to St. Mary, it contains Early English and Decorated work, with an effigy of a priest popularly called "Grandfather Greybeard." There are several brasses, 1368-1594, and an excellent wooden roof.

Photograph] **Leighton Buzzard Church.** [*H. A. Strange.*
With Early English Tower and Spire.

PLACES EASILY REACHED BY RAILWAY.

Leighton Buzzard. The church is dedicated to All Saints. The tower and spire and a great deal of the interior is Early English and Early Decorated, the windows are mostly Perpendicular. On the west door is remarkable ironwork by Thomas de Lightone. The magnificent spire showing well marked entasis or slight outward curving, is a landmark for many miles around. There is a Perpendicular Market Cross in the Market Place. The little church, dedicated to St. Leonard, at Heath, two miles to the north, is modern. At two and a-half miles north of the town, at Reach, is a large pit dug in boulder clay with glacially striated stones.

Luton. The beautiful and interesting church is dedicated to St. Mary. The architecture is Decorated and Perpendicular, within there is a remarkable baptistery, and a chapel known as the Wenlock Chapel. There is a much worn stone rood stair and many notable tombs, monuments, and brasses.

Luton Hoo. The station is named after the adjoining Luton Hoo Park and Mansion. The word Hoo is a personal one, and indicates the name of the ancient owners, it is an ancient form of Hill, usually spelt Hoe as in Totternhoe. There is a pleasant country walk, close to the Lea, on the east side of the railway to Harpenden, on the Great Northern.

Harpenden. The church is dedicated to St. Nicholas, and, with the exception of the tower, has been at various times rebuilt—the last time in 1862, in imitation of Early Decorated work. The original church was late Norman. The font is Norman. There are several brasses—one of kneeling figures—to William Cressy and his wife, 1558-1571; another to William Annabull and wife, 1441.

Wheathampstead. The church is dedicated to St. Helen; it is partly Early English, and contains fine carving, effigies, and monuments. A rude semicircular arch, filled in with masonry, in the exterior of the south transept wall, is probably Saxon.

South-east of the ancient village is a long and deep ditch, called the Devil's Dyke. One mile south is a fine extensive common or heath, called No-Man's-land ; in the upper pale, sandy gravel Palæolithic implements occur.   The whole district is rich in Neolithic implements.

Ayot. This name has been spelt in various ways in the past ; it means an island, and refers to elevated ground, formerly surrounded by swamp from the Lea.   The church of Ayot St. Peter is a quarter mile north of the railway-station ; the ancient church has gone : a new one was built on the old site in the last century, and was replaced by a third in 1862.   This was burnt in 1874, and a fourth built in 1875.   There is a beautiful walk by road from Ayot to Welwyn, one and a-half miles.   After passing through the brickfield, the road can be taken either to the left or right of Homer's Wood.   Paleolithic implements may be found in the gravel-pits at or near Welwyn.

Ayot St. Lawrence is two miles north-west of Ayot St. Peter.   The old church is a ruin, but some monuments remain.   The new church is in imitation of Greek work, and was built in 1778.

Hatfield. The church is dedicated to St. Etheldreda ; it is cruciform in plan, with a central tower and spire, chiefly of Decorated date, with a little Transitional work.   The Cecil and Ponsbourne Chapels contain monuments of the Cecils, Brockets, and Reades. Hatfield became the property of the Cecils, by exchange, in 1603, when James I. gave Hatfield to Sir Robert Cecil for Theobalds, on the Essex side of Herts.   The house was built between 1605 and 1611.   There are several unusually large oaks—one called the *lion*—in the park, and a remarkable garden of clipped yews called the *vineyard*.

Places usually selected for Driving.

Ashridge. There is no excursion by road from Dunstable that can equal in wild, romantic beauty, that along the Icknield Way, at the foot of Dunstable Downs to Ivinghoe and Ashridge.   Ivinghoe, five miles, village of Aldbury, eight miles.   The way is by West Street to Well Head and the " Plough " Inn. At the " Plough " the road to the right leads to Eaton

Specially drawn] **Aldbury, showing the Stocks and Whipping Post.** [by Duncan Moul.

Bray and Edlesborough that to the left to Dagnall, an alternative way to Ashridge. Proceeding along the Icknield Way, Edlesborough Hill and Bibsall Spring are passed on the right, till cross roads are reached at the "Travellers' Rest" Inn, the road to the right leads to Edlesborough, that to the left to Dagnall. At this point the Icknield Way is obliterated, the road to Combe Hole is—although incorrectly named "Icknield Way" on the large scale Ordnance Maps—a comparatively new one made in 1798. Standing at the "Travellers' Rest" and looking towards Beacon Hill, the Icknield Way, previous to 1798, crossed the field to the left from the angle of the cross roads, passed to the left of Gallow's Hill, and quarter of a-mile south of the highest point of Ivinghoe Beacon. It then passed to Waterloo Farm on the left, with Pitstone on the right. At half-a-mile before reaching Pitstone from Ivinghoe, the true Icknield Way is again reached. From the "Travellers' Rest" the track of the old way can be clearly seen over a depression on Ivinghoe Hill, south of the highest point. At less than a mile from the inn, on the road to Beacon Hill is a deep coombe, depression or gorge on the right, known as Coombe Hole; accidents have occurred at this spot. There is a spring at the bottom of the coombe. The hill on the left is Gallow's Hill. In driving, Beacon Hill is usually rounded to the left, to what was once Ivinghoe Common also on the left, to Ringshall, Ringshall Lodge, and Little Gaddesden. The hill on the right is called Witchcraft Hill and the valley Witchcraft Bottom. At Ringshall, or through Ashridge Park, at Little Gaddesden, the village of Aldbury, with its stocks and whipping-post, is usually made for. Brakes laden with excursionists and motor cars are refused admittance to Ashridge Park. There is little need for any visitor to wish to enter the park, as the adjoining country is equally, if not more beautiful and certainly more romantically wild. Box trees in a wild state occur. Favourite places of resort are "the monument," a land-mark from the North-Western Railway, Wards Coombe, Duncombe Terrace, Steps Hill, Berkhampstead Common, and Aldbury. A very long day, or several days may be enjoyably spent in the neighbourhood of Ashridge Park ; drivers from Dunstable know all the roads perfectly well ; traps usually put up at Aldbury. Only accommodation and refreshments, such as are to be met with in villages, can be obtained ; holiday-makers are therefore advised to take their own refreshments from Dunstable. Tea, ginger-beer and buns can be obtained close to the Bridgewater Monument. The return journey can be made through the village of Ivinghoe. Half-a-mile before the village is reached, the road on the left is the Icknield Way, its course on the right as already stated over Beacon Hill, has been obliterated. Just after passing Beacon Hill, the road to the left leads to the ancient village of Ivinghoe Aston, where numerous Roman remains have been found, including red, lustrous pottery, stamped ALBANVS. Or Dunstable may be reached by way of Ringshall, Dagnall, and Valence End Farm to the "Plough" Inn. At Dagnall Roman vases have been found and pottery stamped NICEPHORVS. All the ways are romantically wild and beautiful.

Visitors sometimes extend their drive through Aldbury to these places, two and a-half **Tring and** miles from Aldbury Church, past Tring **Tring Park.** railway-station—a beautiful drive. Close to one of the entrances to Tring Park is the instructive Natural History Museum, established by the Hon. Walter Rothschild. It is open to the public on week-day afternoons.

A drive from Ivinghoe is sometimes made to this village, close to which is the Buckingham- **Aston-Clinton.** shire seat of Lord Battersea, formerly, when Mr. Cyril Flower, M.P. for South Beds. The distance is ten or eleven miles from Dunstable, and four or five beyond the Chiltern Hills at Ivinghoe. The chief inducement to visit the village has been political and sentimental. There is, however, an Early English church, with Decorated chancel, piscina, and sedilia. The word "Faithful," cut in the turf on the hill-side, long marked the grave of a shepherd of that name, who was buried on a position where he was wont to sit and look after his sheep. The place was called the "shepherd's grave."

The Bridgewater Monument in Ashridge Park.

Excursions are sometimes made by road to these places, fifteen or sixteen miles from **Bletchley and Bletchley Park**. Dunstable. Bletchley can be easily and quickly reached by the north-western railway. It is a pleasant country excursion through Leighton Buzzard, on low ground in the valley of the Ouzel.

Photograph]   **At Ashridge.**   *[H. A. Strange.*

A pleasant and favourite drive from Dunstable is to **Woburn**. Woburn, Woburn Park, and Woburn Sands. The distance is eight or nine miles, and the direct way is through Hockliffe, or a pleasanter but longer way is through Chalgrave, Toddington, Milton Bryant and Eversholt. The Dunstable drivers know the roads, points of ingress and egress, and the roads that should be kept to in the park. Woburn, the seat of the Duke of Bedford, is celebrated for its gardens, its rhododendrons, and coniferous trees. The mansion contains sculpture and picture galleries; the sculpture is mostly ancient, there is a sarcophagus from Ephesus, with representations of the dragging of the body of Hector round the walls of Troy, a pavement from Hadrian's Villa, and Roman vases found in Woburn park. The pictures are mostly historical portraits of high interest. The church, dedicated to St. Mary, is modern, on an old foundation; there are one or two monuments and a brass to John Morton, 1394. The church and village look painfully new. A walk from Woburn to Woburn Sands Station, on the north-western railway, through Fir-tree wood, is very beautiful.

The pleasantest way to reach these magnificent chalk **Barton Hills.** hills is by road through Leagrave, Bramingham, and Streatley. It is about eight miles to the village of Barton, where horses can be put up, and village refreshment obtained. The hills are south of the village, the highest is Ravensburgh Castle, a large earthwork, 500 feet above the sea. The downs are celebrated for the characteristics belonging to Dunstable Downs, their altitude, the soft, elastic, fragrant turf, the health-giving air, and the traces of pre-historic and ancient occupation, the most perfect of the latter being the oblong earthern camp, named Ravensburgh Castle. The Barton Hills are rich in rare plants, it is the home of the Pasque Flower, *Anemone Pulsatilla*. In plantations near the hills, the Columbine grows wild. On the hills and on chalky roadside banks numerous orchids may be found, the Bee Orchis in some places appears in large companies, the Fly Orchis grows in bushy places, whilst the Burnt Orchis sometimes appears in thousands. The flora is altogether rich. The church is interesting, and dedicated to St. Nicholas, of Early English and Decorated date, but like nearly every other church mentioned in this little book over-restored. There is a fine wooden roof, and a half-length fourteenth, fifteenth century brass, and another a century later.

L

CHAPTER XIII.

———

Traditions and Proverbial Phrases regarding Dunstable.

A POPULAR tradition affirms that Dunstable or Dunstaple was so named by Henry I. in commemoration of a Saxon soldier or robber named Dun, Dunn, Dunne, or Dunning, who survived the Battle of Hastings and retreated with fifty fol-**Dun the Robber.** lowers to the hills and woods close to where Dunstable now stands. The first syllable of the word is made to represent the outlaw's name, and the latter to represent a suppositious underground cave or *stable* to which he retreated with his horse in times of difficulty The variant *staple* is made to refer to a staple driven into a stake within the stable or cave, by means of which, and a ring, Dun is supposed to have secured his horse.

In the tradition Dun is described as a Saxon soldier, an outlaw, highway robber, burglar, and murderer. He lived with a gang of desperate followers in the woods, like Robin Hood. The gang is reported to have spared neither man, woman, or child, they plundered on the highway and in houses, and spared nothing and no one. When attempts were made to rout or capture Dun, the latter dispersed his assailants and hanged his prisoners on trees, as warnings to law-abiding folk against attacking law-breakers. The robbers changed clothes with the robbed and murdered, and in these clothes masqueraded as well-to-do citizens. The country side at length rose in arms against Dun, and a hundred-and-fifty recruits, armed with pitchforks, scythes, and rakes made an attack upon him and his fifty followers. The object was to secure the leader, but Dun, mounted upon a powerful horse, and armed with a sword, dashed through the crowd of rustics, cutting right and left with his weapon. He was pulled from his horse, but again mounting and again slashing with his sword, escaped. His assailants had now increased in number to three hundred, and with their rude weapons again tore Dun from his horse. The horse at this juncture escaped, and the robber fought single-handed on foot and fought and ran for two miles. Dun lost neither courage or strength and remained unsubdued. Coming to the river Ouse, the outlaw threw off his clothes, and putting his sword in his mouth, plunged into the water and made for the other side. To his surprise he saw the opposite bank covered with new opponents, so that he was unable to land. He now swam down the middle of the stream followed by his would-be captors in boats. He took refuge on a small island, but his pursuers followed and knocked him down by repeated blows on the head, with their oars, and so captured him.

After Dun's serious wounds had been attended to by a surgeon, he was taken, under a strong guard, to Bedford, and, without trial, led to be hanged. Dun fought with his executioners on the scaffold, and nine times overthrew them before his strength was exhausted. The tradition states that the hangmen or headsmen were at length able to chop off both hands of the outlaw, and then both arms at the elbows and shoulders ; next, his feet were chopped off at the ankles, knees, and thighs ; and at length the head was severed from the trunk and burnt. Finally, the different parts of the body were sent to various stations in Bedfordshire, and exhibited as warnings to evil-doers.

A variant of the latter part of the tradition asserts that Henry I., whilst travelling in South Bedfordshire, came upon Dun's gang near where Dunstable now is. The ruffians fled on the approach of the king. Henry I. then caused a pole or pile to be erected in the highway, and affixed his own ring of gold to the pile by an iron staple. This was done to see if any local thief dare steal the king's ring. Both the ring and staple were, however, stolen, and the thief was traced to a house at Houghton Regis, adjoining Dunstable inhabited by a " widow Dun." Dun the robber with ring and staple, was captured in his mother's house, and ultimately hanged.

The tradition is, undoubtedly, old, and perhaps dates from the time of Henry I., but there is no MS. account of Dun older than the middle of the fifteenth century. The legend seems to be founded on the ancient arms of the Priory and Borough. The triangle which depends from the top of the Dunstable shield of arms, is heraldically termed a pile, and is the origin of the king's pole or pile of the tradition. Fixed to the " pile " is a horseshoe, which resembles in shape a " staple," and does duty for a staple in the tradition. Hanging from this staple is an annulet, or ring of gold, the king's ring of the fable.

A cellar, cut in the chalk, under the pavement and slightly under the road, belonging to one of the houses on the west side of Middle Row, is traditionally said to be the cellar, or stable, of Dun. It is also fabulously stated that a stake, with staple and ring, once existed in the cellar. The only fact is, the existence of a cellar, cut out of the chalk and used for tradesmen's boxes, when I was in it a few years ago. The same cellar is popularly stated to lead to a subterranean passage under the road to the Priory or Church. No such passage exists or has ever existed, and there is no masonry of any kind in the cellar.

A certain queen made a wager with a certain king that she would encamp an army within a **Maiden Bower.** bull's hide, the king accepted the wager, but the odds are not mentioned in the tradition. The queen thereupon carefully cut a bull's hide into extremely narrow shreds almost as thin as thread. These she dexterously joined together end to end, and, with the assistance of her maids, drew the thread out as a long attenuated line in Maiden-Bower field. She then bade her maids to carefully form a circle with the thread in their hands. When the thread formed a thin circle on the grass the queen ordered an army to march inside. This the army did, and the king was so struck with admiration and amazement at the queen's skill that he ordered the soldiers to throw up a high bank of chalk on the circular line of the thread, so that the queen's skill might be remembered for ever. Such is a traditional origin of Maiden-Bower. A somewhat similar story is told of Bulverhithe, near Hastings.

Totternhoe. A local tradition of Totternhoe states that the village was once a capital town, and possessed sixteen churches ; this possibly refers to sixteen Roman shrines the place may have once possessed.

Markyate Street Cell. The mansion called the Markyate Street Cell has three times been destroyed by fire, and local tradition has it, that the fires were caused by a " wicked Lady Ferrers," whose apparition was not only seen at the time of the fires, but long afterwards until quite recent times, when a party of young folks were terrified at the apparition in the day-time, during a children's tea. According to old folk's tales the ghost of the lady is seen in the park, generally running, but often swinging from branches of trees and from branch to branch, sometimes, indeed, careering over the tree-tops, and always crying, " God help me." A keeper is reported to have once shot at the clearly visible ghost, but without effect.

It is said that in the year 1840 many farm workmen saw the apparition swinging from a sycamore tree, and so positive were they of the reality of the ghostly presence that they sawed off the branch of the tree, during the absence, and without the permission of the owner.

Tradition says that the " wicked Lady Ferrers " before death was wont to dress in male attire, and, mounted on the back of a coal-black horse with white fore-feet, robbed and maltreated travellers on the high-way near Markyate Street. A variant of the tale says that after death she sometimes imitated the witch and wizard folk and would, in the night, take a farmer's horse and ride it till near daybreak. When her orgie was finished, she would return the horse, exhausted from night gallopping.

Lady Ferrers was, so we are told, at length fatally wounded, and her dead body was found close to an external door of the Markyate Cell. This was a door which was traditionally believed to lead to a secret staircase by which the wicked lady ascended and descended in male dress. After her death, some time before A.D. 1690, the door was built up. After the great fire of 1840 the proprietor of the Cell determined to open this doorway, but not a single Markyate Street man could be got to assist. Workmen were brought from a distance unacquainted with the uncanny business in hand, and when the opening was laid bare a narrow stone staircase was presented to view. The men ascended the steps, but found their progress barred by a stout oaken door. This, by order, was beaten down, but it was afterwards seen that it could have been easily opened by a secret spring, not at first observed. The small chamber to which the stairs led was vacant. A local, almost forgotten, rhyme, says—

> Near the Cell there is a Well,
> Near the Well there is a Tree,
> And under the Tree the Treasure be.

It is perhaps a coincidence that the pre-existing priory or nunnery was given to one George Ferrers, at the time of the dissolution of the religious houses. The lady Ferrers of the ghost story has not been identified.

A long, long time ago, it is said, someone threw a large box of money into the Money-pit, near the great Knoll on Totternhoe Hill. **The Money-pit.** That was at a time when the pit was very much deeper than now. In an old children's game that used to be played there, the youngsters would run nine times round the sloping side of the hollow, and then suddenly jump to the lower part. At that instant the money would always be heard to chink at the bottom. Since then, rubbish has been thrown into the hole to make it shallower and less dangerous. The money-pit is probably the mouth of a Bronze-age store-pit. There may be a grain of truth in the tradition, and possibly bronzes—not money—may be below.

Of the larger Roman Ditch on Totternhoe Camp, a local tradition says "soldiers dug it." There were originally eight trees planted in this ditch; one has died and been uprooted. Old folks say that eight kings were buried under the trees.

The Five Knolls, on Dunstable Downs, are the traditional burial-places of five kings. By kings is meant chiefs.

The British Hut remains on the brow of Blows Downs, overlooking southern Dunstable **Oliver Cromwell.** (*See map*) were considered by the rustics of my boyhood's time to be places made by Oliver Cromwell in which he fixed his cannons when he came to Dunstable to blow down Dunstable Church— a mythical event referred to by no historian. In the chalk pit which then existed a little below the hut remains, the chalk was full of horizontal and vertical fissures; these fissures were said to have been caused by the repeated explosions of Cromwell's powerful artillery.

Matthew Paris speaks of the martyr St. Katharine as Sancta Katerina. It is singular that the **Saint Katherine and Saint Frehemund.** festival of St. Katherine still faintly survives in this district near Ashridge and Wigginton. The country-folk there sometimes visit each other with small presents to "keep Katerin," which is the form of the word given by Paris. Sometimes the word is varied to " Kattern." The remembrance of St. Frehemund is still commemorated by the Dunstable May fair, as instituted by King John. (See p. 90.)

A tradition existed when I was a boy that Dunstable Church was first built on the hill above Pascombe Pit. A tradition still exists that Edlesborough Church was first built on Edlesborough Hill, overlooking Bibshall Spring. The name Bibshall now only exists traditionally, and no one knows where Bibba's Hall stood. There is Dagnall and Hudnall near by.

In both the Dunstable and Edlesborough traditions, the stones of the original churches are stated to have been removed at night by fairies. Probably stones belonging to Roman shrines of some kind were removed to form part of the new churches. I have, however, seen no Roman work or Roman tiles in either of the churches. The earth has been disturbed on Edlesborough Hill.

PROVERBIAL PHRASES IN REGARD TO DUNSTABLE.

"As black as a Dunstable Crow." This probably refers to Dunstable Rooks, which are remarkably **Proverbial Phrases.** abundant near Dunstable, they appear unusually black when seen in contrast with the arable fields of chalk.

"Dunstable Crows." These are really Royston Crows, a pied or greyish variety of the common black crow. The phrase is distinct from "as black as a Dunstable Crow." Dunstable or Royston Crows are traditionally said to have been unknown before coaching times and to have practically gone away again with the coaches. In coaching times they are said to have been unusually abundant, they were caught in large numbers, and cooked at the "Sugar Loaf" and "Crown" Hotels. These Royston Crows were sent to London in a cooked state and sold in large numbers, they were not eaten much in Dunstable.

"Downright Dunstable." Sir Walter Scott says, in *Red Gauntlet* Chap. XVII.—"If this is not plain speaking there is no such place as downright Dunstable." This saying is often supposed to refer to the honest outspoken people of the town, but it is really a punning reference to the approach to the town by the Roman Road from the South, "down" referring to the descent and "right" being used in the sense of straight. In other words, Dunstable is approached by a straight descending road.

"Silly Houghton." Houghton in Domesday Book is termed a Royal Demesne Manor, it is still Houghton Regis or the King's Houghton. Henry I. built his palace in what at that time was Houghton. Thereupon Houghton was termed Sælig Houghton, which means fortunate Houghton in the sense of being a Royal Manor at the time of the Conqueror, and afterwards having a palace of the Conqueror's son within its boundaries. Silly is a modern corruption of sælig,—fortunate, happy.

"Tring, Wing and Ivinghoe." The earliest authority for the rhyme :—

> " Tring, Wing and Ivingo
> The (these) Hampden did forgo
> For striking of a blow
> And glad he could 'scape so,"

is in the return made by John Yale, rector of Great Hampden to Willis's circular of interrogations, 1712. Yale says : "There is an antient Tradition of King Edward 3rd and his son Edward, the black prince's being entertained at Hampden. But the Prince and Hampden exercising themselves in feats of Chivalry, they differed and grew so hot that Hampden struck the Prince on the face, which made the King and prince go away in great wrath upon which came this rhyme."

The story is fiction made to fit an old rhyme, the lines are probably from a royalist ballad and indicate that Hampden must be dislodged, and Tring, Wing and Ivinghoe held by the royalists. There are many modern variants of the rhyme. Sir Walter Scott borrowed the last of the three place-names for his novel *Ivanhoe*, and printed the stanza in his preface, somewhat incorrectly, as he wrote from local tradition.

The neighbourhood of Dunstable has long been celebrated for its Sky-larks. They breed **Dunstable Larks.** on and near the hills in vast numbers, and their singing often fills the air with music. Professional "larkers" catch them in nets of a large size, sometimes carried by two men. In the season the larkers start work at seven o'clock in the evening and return at one or two o'clock in the morning. They can catch from 300 to 400 larks in one night, and often take birds of a much larger size. They send the larks to London, some alive in small cages, others dead for the poultry shops. There is practically no call for them now in Dunstable, although the demand is said to have been great at the hotels and inns in coaching days. If the London demand could be made to cease, the Downs at Dunstable would not be defaced by lark-catching vagrants. It is locally reported that about 50,000 Dunstable larks are sent to London annually.

CHAPTER XIV.

Local Folk=Lore and Superstition.

THERE are four very narrow old-time passages at Dunstable—three from the High Street and one from Church Street. Two communicate on the **Old Passages at Dunstable.** west between Ashton Street and High Street. The one on the east, which leads to the church, is named "Church Alley." A little way up this passage is a branch which leads into Church Street, named "Little Alley." In the old times before gas was introduced these passages were disliked in the dark winter nights, and "Church Alley," which led to the churchyard, was avoided by the superstitious as much as possible. Old Dunstable folk are reported to have walked in the road or ran by this passage on dark nights.

There is a persistent belief amongst some old local village **The Hare.** folk that if a hare runs through a village it presages fire; that some hares can make themselves suddenly invisible, even when close by a spectator; that certain bad men and women can change themselves into hares, and from hares back again into bad men and women.

Witches, or bad women, can change themselves into cats. These cats quietly leave villages and meet folk **The Cat.** coming from market or from church or chapel; they walk near the villagers in the cat-form, and listen to what they are talking about—afterwards they make use of the information gained for bad purposes.

The belief in witches has nearly died out, but believers who still survive find support for their superstition from **Witches.** certain Bible texts which they quote when remonstrated with. I have heard of several reputed witches who once lived in villages near Dunstable. The men, who were afraid of them, dared not refuse them anything they asked for, usually part of a dinner, part of a man's ale or small sums of money. I have, however, only been able to secure the name of one witch, viz.: Trinity. As the witch Trinity is asserted to have lived in different villages some distance apart it would appear that the name was really first applied as a magical exclamation or exorcism. It was perhaps in old times a religious superstition that the mere mention of the name of the Trinity would baffle a malignant enchanter.

It was popularly believed in villages till recent times that " Night-Hags " or " Folk " got into farmer's stables **Night-Hags.** at night, loosened the horses and galloped them over the fields, till near sunrise. Before dawn these " Folk " or " Leather-coats " returned the horses to their stalls. Sometimes the " Folk " loosened the horses and hunted them about all night in the stables. The proof existed in the fact of the horses being found badly sweating in the morning. Bad ventilation of the stable, then as now, never appears to have presented itself to the rustic mind. The horses, it is said, could see the " Hags," " Folk," or " Leather-coats," but human beings, as a rule, could not. If a horse suddenly stopped in a road or field it was thought that a " Leather-coat " was near by and had terrified the horse. No amount of scolding or whipping could make a horse pass an invisible " Leather-coat " till the latter thought proper to move off. Some old workmen have told me that they have seen these " Night-Hags," " Folk," or " Leather-coats " sitting under trees or looking over gates, but when approached they always went out of sight. Some old men have told me they have actually seen these apparitions " turn invisible."

Another belief is that there are ghostly black dogs, the size of large retrievers, about in the fields at night, that these dogs are generally near gates and stiles, and are of such a forbidding aspect that no one dare venture to pass them, and that it means death to shout at them. In some places the black spectral dog is named "Shuck" and is said to be headless.

Spectral Animals. There is a Dog's-Bank at Totternhoe, which reminds one of the She-Wolf's Cairn, Carnedd-y-Filiast, on the mountain top between Bala and Yspytty.

There is a belief in a black pig that is seen in high roads and can never be caught. Whips and sticks are said to pass through it without effect, and that it becomes lost in hedges or under horses' feet. One man pursued it to a closed field-gate, through which it passed. At the moment of passing through, a white-faced spectral man within the field, and, with arms folded on the top rail of the gate, stared into the pursuer's face and vanished.

It is considered wicked to mention the numbers which **Stars.** make a group or constellation of stars, and that it is very wicked to attempt to count stars, or even to point at them.

It is wicked during a snow-storm to say it is "old **Snow and** Mother Christmas picking her geese" **Thunder Storms.** —because it is God who sends the snow.

It is wicked to make any trivial remark during a thunderstorm, because God is then speaking to the wicked.

At certain village weddings the cottage doors from **Weddings.** which the bride and bridegroom emerge are kept carefully fixed open till the return of the bridal party.

It is common for some villagers to burn lamps, candles, or nightlights at night; the light is believed to keep ghosts at a distance, as ghosts are averse to lights.

Ghosts are still believed in; they are chiefly seen sitting **Ghosts.** on rails in churchyards. A village man once reported to me that he had just seen Satan; the man himself was nearly dead with terror. A few folk still believe that Satan is about at night. He has been reported as seen sitting down by the road-side, and looking out of the window of a deserted cottage just before sunrise.

It was extensively believed that the old Market Hall at Dunstable was haunted. The most circumstantial stories were prevalent before the destruction of the building by fire.

It is considered very unlucky to meet a funeral; **Funerals.** village folk will sometimes turn and slowly accompany the procession for a short distance and let it outwalk them. Wherever a funeral has passed establishes a right of way, and a church-way or church-yard way can never be stopped.

It was an old Bedfordshire custom to immure and preserve the best clothes of a dead person, so that the best clothes might be ready on the Resurrection Day.

If there is an unusual amount of illness in a village, it **Illness.** is said to be because it is the breeding-time of lions, and lions only breed once in seven years.

If a person lies dead on a Sunday, or if a grave is **Death.** open on a Sunday, another person in the village is certain to die before the week is out.

Parsley must never be dug up and transplanted; if this is done it invariably happens that there is serious illness in the house for a year. Cuttings or seeds must be used for new growths.

If the rope wheezes when the bell is tolled for the dead, it is certain that some other dead person will be tolled for within a week.

Persons who had committed suicide in Dunstable were, **Suicide.** within the memory of old people now living, not buried in the churchyard, but near the Priory wall, outside the west end of the church. Others were buried in the middle of the town where the main roads cross. Still others at the cross roads at the end of West Street. In the thirteenth century, according to the *Annales*, the bodies of suicides were "projected" into a ditch.

It is believed that certain domestic animals will bring bad luck to a family, and that bad luck will continue to pursue the family whilst the animal is kept. Sometimes valuable dogs are shot on this account only.

It was not uncommon fifty years ago to fix the blade of a dinner-knife between the bricks of the brick-floor of cottages close to the threshold. The embedded knife was considered equal to preventing the entry of any bad character to the cottage. Sometimes a horse-shoe was so embedded, the arms upward, if **Luck.** downward it would be useless as all the virtue would run out. Some rustics say that horseshoes are no good unless they have been worn by stallions. Should a cottage be visited by a strange witch-like woman or bad character of any sort, it was the custom to observe where the feet of the intruder had been planted. On the departure of the suspected visitor, a cross was made with a knife on the footprint, or on the place where the feet had been; it was then believed that the intruder could never return. The efficacy of this act might be tested after a visit from a tax-gatherer.

It is considered very unlucky to see a single crow or rook. Rustics say, "Oh, there's a crow: spit on the ground." It is said that one crow is bad luck, two good luck, three signify a wedding, four a funeral.

Stones with holes are believed to bring good luck. I have often been asked for the gift, from my collection, of a stone with a hole through it. A man once brought me a large flint so perforated and said it had been "hanging in a stable for many years." "What for"? I asked. "To prevent horses from sweating," he replied. The stone, without doubt, had originally been hung up as a charm against visits from the "Night-Hag."

It is believed by some, even now, that the water at **Miraculous** Well-head, near Totternhoe, will cure sore **Cures.** eyes and strengthen weak ones.

House-leek on a roof, it is supposed by some, will prevent a farm from being fired by lightning, and a root of plantain, with a small piece of coal attached, will prevent any person from being struck by lightning.

Stewed earth-worms are regarded by some as a cure for jaundice ; and a live garden-snail kept in a large pill-box in the pocket will, it is said, cure tooth-ache.

A skinned and fried mouse is still regarded as a certain cure for whooping-cough. I have never met with any superstitious beliefs regarding the shrew-mouse, so common elsewhere.

Clippings from the dark cross on a donkey's shoulder are considered potent for good, because the knee of Jesus rested there when he rode into Jerusalem. I have known the clippings to be wrapped in paper and tied under a child's foot as a cure for whooping-cough.

Grottoes. Fifty years ago it was a custom of Dunstable boys to build grottoes of oyster-shells, lighted within by candles, on August 5th, St. James's day. The grottoes were placed at street-corners. The memory of the shrine of St. James the Greater, at Composte la, and of pilgrims with shells attached to their coats or hats, had, however, long been forgotten.

Bonfires. Old folks, sixty years ago, when I was a boy, could just remember, bonfires lit on the downs on June 24th, in honour of midsummer.

May-Pole May Day. The may-pole only exists as a tradition ; there is a May-pole yard in West Street, Dunstable. Sixty years ago the May-day festival was kept by dancing in masquerade in the streets. May-day is still kept in some of the villages, as at Edlesborough, but the festival is fast dying out. Young girls carry dolls embowered with flowers in litters or perambulators, usually covered with white sheeting. The girls take the dolls and flowers—called the " May garland "— from house to house, remove the sheeting, and sing of the happiness of May. Half a century ago there was, in addition to this, a procession of young girls, carrying sticks garlanded with flowers ; these were called " May-dancers."

Breeding Stones. Amongst farmer's men generally stones are believed to breed. The men say it does not matter how many stones are gathered from the fields during one season, there are always the same number the next year, so they must breed.

Pieces of Plum-pudding stone—collections of pebbles naturally fixed together as if with cement—the Hertfordshire Conglomerate of geologists—are said to be "breeders."   I once remonstrated with a man, and, pointing to a large block of Conglomerate by a gate-side, said, "That block has been there for twenty years to my knowledge, and has never bred."   The man replied—"Breeding stones are exactly like taters; they breed in the ground, not by the side of gates."

Many years ago—a century or more—a man named
Blood Tokens. Cain was murdered in a field named Bob's Acre, two or three fields to the north of Leagrave March farm.   When the dead body was discovered it was carried to the "Horse Shoe" inn, Leagrave.   Whilst the body was at the inn, the suspected murderer was found and taken to the inn to touch the body.   Immediately on doing so, it is said that the blood poured from the wound in a stream and soaked the brick floor.   On trial, this suspected murderer—one Nott by name—was convicted and hanged at Gib-Acre, by Dray's Ditches, near Bramingham.   On being requested to plead, Nott is reported to have replied, "I am Nott, the man."   In the memory of my father, the reputed blood-stains were constantly exhibited at the inn; it was asserted that the stains could not be scrubbed from the bricks, and that on being damped the bricks "sweated blood."

In Tilsworth Churchyard there is a gravestone on
The Blackgrove Wood Murder. the right of the entrance-gate with the following inscription :—

"This Stone was erected by Subscription to the Memory of a Female unknown found murdered in Blackgrove Wood. Aug. 15th, 1821.

 Oh, pause my friend, and drop the silent tear,
 Attend and learn why I was buried here.
 Perchance some distant earth had held my clay,
 If I'd outlived the sad, the fatal day.
 To you unknown, my case not understood,
 From whence I came, or why in Blackgrove Wood,
 This truth's too clear, and nearly all that's known,
 I there was murdered and the Villain flown.
 May God, whose piercing eye pursues his flight,
 Pardon the crime, but bring the deed to light."

There is no record in the Church register. The body of the girl, who was a stranger, was found with her throat cut against the trunk of a tree. This tree is still alive, and is well known. Its position in Blackgrove Wood is shown by the small cross on the map. The murderer was never brought to justice, but the name of the suspected man is well known in the villages of Tilsworth and Stanbridge.

It is asserted by some people even at the present day that human blood has welled up from the foot of the tree ever since the murder was committed. A variant says that human blood has oozed from a hole in the trunk. It is certain that many unwelcome excursionists still make pilgrimages to the tree. The writer of these lines has never seen any blood-like stain on the ground or any red sap oozing from the tree, but several persons have most positively assured him that they have seen the " blood-stains." The farmer who rents the wood says there was certainly at one time a natural hole in the trunk of the tree, from which red sap ran, but the wound is now grown over with bark.

If a person is found dead near the roadside, in the neighbourhood of villages near Dunstable, **The Sign of the Cross.** it is customary to cut a somewhat large cross in the turf as near as possible to the place where the body was found. Sometimes the cross is incised in the trunk of a tree, if one happens to be near. About four years ago there was a large cross of this kind cut in the turf by the high road near Kensworth Lynch. A few years before there was a cross cut in the turf in Caddington Lane, near the brickmakers' cottages. This was, later on, replaced by an incised cross on an adjoining tree-trunk.

All the commoner superstitions of spilt salt, crossed knives, Friday, thirteen at table, etc., are frequently met with.

M

CHAPTER XV.

Notes on Local Geology and Natural History.

DUNSTABLE stands on the stratum known to geologists as the Lower Chalk. The higher parts of the town are near the base of the Middle Chalk, and **Geology.** at the highest part of Dunstable Downs there is 80 feet of Upper Chalk. In past times there was fully 300 feet more chalk than now on the top of the Downs, with fossils such as *Micraster cor-anguinum* and *M. cor-testudinarium*. This 300 feet has been partly carried away by glaciers, and partly washed away by the rainfall of hundreds of thousands of years. That it once existed is shown by the characteristic fossils now found on the surface of the ground. Of the Upper Chalk a great deal has been softened and washed away, and the flints and fossils, heavier than chalk-wash, have been left on the present surface.

At the top of Dunstable Downs, where Pascombe Pit is, there is a peculiar form of hard, stony, broken-up chalk, called Chalk Rock by geologists, and " Kerlock " by local rustics. It varies in thickness from four to eight feet, and contains Gasteropoda and green-coated flint nodules. There was formerly 400 feet of Upper Chalk above this stratum. Chalk-Rock, or " Kerlock," was formerly used for mending the roads. It is unusually full of fossils as *Ventriculites, Micraster, Terebratula, Rhynchonella*, and *Inoceramus*.

Beneath this Chalk-Rock is the Middle Chalk ; it is nearly 300 feet deep, and the bottom is on a level with the centre of Dunstable. It contains a few flints and such fossils as *Holaster planus, Terebratula gracilis* and *Rhynchonella Cuvieri*. At the base for about 10 feet the form of chalk named Melbourne Rock is met with, and underneath a distinct 4 feet stratum, containing the fossil named *Belemnitella plena*.

We now come to the Lower Chalk and Chalk Marl beneath Dunstable town. At 80 feet beneath the town surface, Totternhoe stone is met with; there is six to ten feet of it, and on this stratum springs of water occur. Totternhoe stone, at Totternhoe, contains such fossils as *Pecten orbicularis*, but it is very much richer in fossils at Chalton. Sometimes the water is 15 feet above the stone, or 65 feet beneath the surface. Water cannot be got at Dunstable without an excavation of from 65 feet to 80 feet. A characteristic fossil of the Lower Chalk above Totternhoe stone is *Holaster subglobosus*.

Under the Totternhoe stone is Chalk Marl or clay for 90 feet; it, however, undulates and varies in depth from 60 feet to 120 feet. This Chalk Marl is impervious to water, and its characteristic fossil is *Ammonites varians*. The Dunstable Waterworks are excavated into about 35 feet of Chalk Marl. Mr. Bennett's deep well at the Brewery is carried down to 100 feet in the same substance.

At 80 feet under the Totternhoe stone through Chalk Marl the stiff clay called the Gault is met with at Stanbridge Ford; but it is 280 feet at Luton. Messrs. Le Grand and Co. have informed Mr. Bennett that they think the Gault would be reached at Dunstable at 400 feet from the surface ; it had not been reached at 322 feet. The Gault produces coprolite nodules ; characteristic fossils are *Belemnites, Terebratula, Parasmilia, and Lamna*.

Beneath the Gault is the material known as Cambridge Green Sand ; this is really the lowest bed of the chalk. Characteristic fossils are *Sphærodus* and *Acrodus*.

It is not necessary to describe strata beneath the sandy substance at the base of the chalk series. In the deep valley at the foot of Dunstable Downs, stretching from Leighton Buzzard, Eaton Bray, and Stanbridge to

Sewell, the lower strata just mentioned crop up on the surface or are exposed in section—Lower Chalk, Totternhoe Stone, Chalk Marl, Gault and Cambridge Green Sand. In the naturally excavated valley beyond Dunstable one naturally sees on the surface what can only be seen in deep excavations in the town.

The source of the Ver at Markyate Street is about 30 feet above the Totternhoe stone line in the Lower Chalk. The Ouzel at Well Head, is about twelve feet above the stone—the source of the Lea at Leagrave is about thirty feet below the bottom of the stone. When allowance is made for irregularities in stratification these figures show the line of the springs in the neighbourhood of Dunstable. Practically, they are the same as in Dunstable itself.

The Chalk Marl begins at the foot of Dunstable Downs, spreads westward, and includes Sewell, Totternhoe, Edlesborough, and Ivinghoe. The line of Gault begins near Stanbridge Ford railway-station, spreads westwards, and passes to Eatou Bray, then to Ivinghoe-Aston, and the west side of Ivinghoe; it includes Northall. Numerous clay-pits occur in the district, where the stiff grey clay may be seen in section. A stretch of Green Sand occurs between Eaton Bray and Edlesborough, and there is more close to Leighton Buzzard, where large sand-pits may be seen from the Leighton and Dunstable railway. In this sand, large blocks of hard brown Sandstone occur; these have been extensively used as building material in some of the local churches.

The chalk, clay, and sand have represented this part of England for an incalculable number of years—since the time when the whole mass of chalk emerged from the sea as an old sea-bottom. The excavated valleys were once covered with chalk.

There are other deposits of a surface nature on the hill-tops and in the valleys of less age. The older belong to the great Glacial Period, when gravels, boulders, beach pebbles and clays were brought by glaciers to this district from Scotland and Wales. The glacial boulder-clay can be well studied at Reach, near

Leighton Buzzard, where flints and blocks of stone foreign to this district and deeply striated by glacial action can readily be found in the great clay-pit where the material is dug for bricks. On the top of Dunstable Downs, in the direction of Whipsnade and Kensworth, and on Blows Downs, chiefly towards Caddington, are surface deposits of stony clay. Lumps of crystalline quartz, ironstone, Lydian stone, quartzite, and many other blocks of stone, brought from the north, north-north-east and north-west, may be found on the surface of the hills, mixed with flints ploughed out of the chalk by glaciers. Some of the fossils are local, from the chalk series; others are foreign to the district, and brought by glaciers from a distance. Here and there, on the hills and in the valleys, may be seen massive blocks of indurated sandstone, dropped by over-balancing icebergs. Many of these boulders now rest by ditch and field sides; others are in villages and towns—there are several in Dunstable town. The surface material at Whipsnade Heath is termed by geologists Red clay-with-flints; the red clay is merely reddened and softened chalk, and the red colour is caused by the presence above of ironstone. The flints of this material are really chalk flints *in situ*. It will be seen by observation that in some places the red clay changes imperceptibly to chalk, and the same stratum of flints may be in some places in pure chalk, and a little further on in red clay.

Up to this time no human being had ever trodden on the ground where Dunstable now is; but the arctic cold of the Glacial Period gradually passed away, and the climate became warm. At this time Britain was conjoined to the Continent, and hordes of Primeval Men came from Southern Europe, Northern Africa, and Tropical Asia to where Dunstable now is, as described in the chapter on Primeval Man and Beast. The former presence of these Primeval men is chiefly known by the presence of beautifully formed implements of stone deeply embedded in post-Glacial brick earth or rain-washings of the Glacial deposits. The men were nearly all destroyed in floods of mud and water, as already described.

In giving the following lists of Birds and Wild Plants, **Birds.** localities have been omitted ; had localities been printed, they would have led to the speedy total extermination of the rarer species. At and close to Dunstable high and dry and low and wet ground are easy of access. Both are in many places in a state of wild nature. There is also a great variety in the soils—pure chalk, stiff stony clay on the hills, wet chalk marl and gault clay, green sand and boulder clay.

As regards the birds, they are incessantly shot without mercy, chiefly by bird-stuffers with gun-licences. Some of the skins are put into glass cases, others upon hats. Dunstable is too small a place to support a professional bird-stuffer : the depredators chiefly reside in adjoining towns.

The rarer plants are treated in just as bad a way. Idlers, wasters, and hawkers learn where the rarer ferns and flowering plants grow and dig them up for sale or speedy death in unsuitable gardens. The demand regulates the supply, and the people of Dunstable should not purchase stuffed local birds from bird-stuffers or ferns and wild flowering plants from hawkers.

The list of local birds has been made by my grandson, Lawrence R. Smith.

I.—BIRDS.

Falconidæ (Falcons).
> Buzzard.—Partially migratory, harmless,
> Kestrel.—Resident, harmless.
> Peregrine falcon.—Harmless, as in the two last, except in occasional visits to farmyards for chickens,

Strigidæ (Owls),
> Long-eared owl.—Resident, harmless.
> Barn owl.—Resident, harmless.
> Tawny owl.—Resident ; harmless, except, as in the two last, for an occasional rabbit or chicken.

Laniidæ (Shrikes),
> Red-backed shrike.—Migratory, harmless.

Turdidæ (Thrushes),
> Blackbird.—Resident, partly helpful.
> Thrush,—Resident, partly helpful.
> Fieldfare,—Winter visitor, partly helpful.
> Ring Ouzel.—Migratory ; unwelcome near fruit gardens, but partly helpful.
> Missel Thrush.—Resident, partly helpful.
> Red-wing.—Winter visitor, partly helpful.

Sylviidæ (Warblers).
    Hedgesparrow.—Resident, harmless.
    Nightingale.—Migratory, harmless. A local rhyme
      puts into words the song of the nightingale as
      follows :—

        " I've a thorn in my nest,
          And it pricks my poor breast,
        I can get me no rest ;
          Sweet !—jug-a-jug jug ! "

    Robin.—Resident, partly helpful.
    Chiff-Chaff,—Migratory, harmless.
    Golden-crested Wren,—Resident, harmless.
    Redstart.—Migratory, harmless.
    Wheatear.—Spring visitor, farmer's friend.
    Stone-chat.—Farmer's friend.
    White-throat.—Migratory, harmless,
    Lesser White-throat,—Spring visitor, partly helpful.
    Garden Warbler.—Spring visitor ; lover of fruit.
    Black Cap.—Spring visitor, partly helpful.
    Sedge Warbler.

Troglodytidæ (Wrens).
    Wren.—Resident, harmless.

Certhiidæ (Creepers).
    Creeper.—Resident, harmless.

Paridæ (Tits).
    Long-tailed tit.—Resident, harmless.
    Cole tit.—Resident, harmlees.
    Blue tit.—Resident, partly helpful.
    Great tit.—Resident, partly helpful.

Motacillidæ (Wagtails).
    Meadow pipit.
    Pied wagtail.—Resident, harmless.
    Grey wagtail.—Resident, harmless.
    Yellow wagtail.—Resident, harmless.

Alaudidæ (Larks).
    Skylark.—Partly migratory, helpful.

Emberizidæ (Buntings).
    Cirl bunting.
    Resident, partly helpful.
    Yellow hammer.
    Common bunting.—Eater of grain.
    Black-headed bunting, summer visitor.

Fringillidæ (Finches).
    Brambling.
    Bullfinch.—Resident, partly helpful.
    Hawfinch.—Partly migratory ; consumed fruits, seeds,
      berries, peas.
    Chaffinch.—Resident, partly helpful
    Redpoll.—Resident, harmless.
    Goldfinch.—Resident, harmless.

Tree Sparrow.—Locally migratory, winter visitor : consumes grain, seeds, insects, and soft parts of plants.

Linnet.—These are the birds that appear in the fields and sail in the air in thousands soon after harvest-time. Resident, harmless.

Sturnidæ (Starlings).

Starling.—Residents and partly winter visitors ; farmers' friends. These birds congregate in the fields after harvest-time in thousands. Some rustics cruelly split their tongues with thin sixpences in a barbarous effort " to make them talk."

Corvidæ (Crows).

Rook.—Resident ; one of the farmer's best friends.

Carrion Crow.—Resident, farmer's friend.

Royston Crow.—Resident, farmer's friend. Rook and crow pies are made in the Dunstable district ; but the flesh of the birds is black and bitter and not approved by all. The bad taste is caused by the putrid filth on which the birds feed ; dead and rotten rats are much approved by crows. Rooks are shot at intervals at the rookeries, and small parcels of about six birds are tied together, and sent as presents to friends of the sportsmen.

Raven.—This bird occasionally flies over Dunstable : it flies at a considerable height, and has a loud cry, but unlike the crow. It is partly migratory and partly helpful.

Magpie.—Partly helpful.

Jackdaw.—One of the farmer's best friends.

Jay. Partly helpful.

Hirundinidæ (Swallows).

Martin.—Migratory, harmless.

Sand Martin.—Migratory, harmless.

Swallow.—Migratory, harmless.

Cypselidæ (Swifts).

Swift.—Migratory, harmless.

Caprimulgidæ (Goatsuckers).

Night-jar or Goatsucker.—Migratory, harmless.

Cuculidæ (Cuckoos).

Cuckoo.—Migratory, harmless.

Alcedinidæ (Kingfishers).

Kingfisher.

Picidæ (Woodpeckers).

Nuthatch.—Resident, partly helpful.

Green Woodpecker.—Resident, harmless.

Columbridæ (Pigeons).

Wood Pigeons.—Resident. These are caught by local rustics with the lure of a dummy pigeon. Sometimes a dead pigeon is used. The example is fixed upright on the ground, its head supported in a small forked branch. This lure never fails to attract other pigeons. Pigeon-catchers can shoot fifty or sixty in a day.

Phasianidæ (Pheasants).
> Pheasant —Troublesome in and near gardens. These birds feed on grain, seeds, worms, insects, caterpillars, etc.
> Partridge (Red-legged, or French Partridge).— These birds feed on grain, etc., as in the last. Both birds are specially fond of ant's eggs.

Rallidæ (Rails).
> Landrail or Corncrake.—Summer visitor, partly helpful.
> Coot.—Partly migratory.
> Moorhen (water-hen).—These often fly at night with loud cries.
> Water-rail.—Often fly at night. The eggs are esteemed by some for the table.

Charadriidæ (Plovers).
> Golden Plover.
> Lapwing or Pewit.—Resident, harmless.

Scolopacidæ (Snipes).
> Common Snipe.
> Redshank
> Curlew.

Laridæ (Gulls).
> Gull. These white birds often appear in large numbers in the fields. They eat the same food as the rooks, chiefly worms and grubs.

Podicipedidæ (Grebes).
> Little Grebe or Dabchick.

Ardeidæ (Herons).
> Heron. } In past times highly esteemed for the table.
> Bittern. }
> There is no heronry now near Dunstable, but the birds rarely breed in solitary nests

Anatidæ (Ducks).
> Wild Duck
> Widgeon.—-Winter visitor. } In past times highly esteemed for the table, the first flies at night, in companies of from three to five.
> Teal.—Winter visitor.
> Wild Goose.—Often flies at night, from one large piece of water to another, in companies of about five or six.

II.—WILD PLANTS.

Plants. The chalk hills are famous for their Orchids. The following may, in their seasons, always be found, some abundantly :—

Orchis pyramidalis, O. ustulata, Gymnadenia canopsea, Ophrys apifera, O. muscifera, Spiranthes autumnalis, Listera ovata, Cephalanthera grandifolia, C. pallens.

Other orchids are frequently in moist pastures, or on

clay soil, as Orchis Morio, O. mascula, O. latifolia, O. maculata, Habenaria viridis, H. chlorantha, Neottia Nidus-avis, Epipactis latifolia.

The following are a few of the less common plants of the district round Dunstable. A notable and most beautiful plant of the chalk hills is Anemone pulsatilla. In woods and meadows are the two Hellebores, H. viridis and H. fœtidus and Aquilegia vulgaris. In the Lea and Ouse, the two water-lilies—Nymphæa alba and Nuphar lutea. The poppies are Papaver Rhœas, P. Lecoqii, P. dubium, and P. Argemone. In boggy places, Drosera rotundifolia, Parnassia palustris, Pinguicula vulgaris. In fields and hedges, Geranium pratense, Adoxa Moschatellina, Hippurus vulgaris, Carum Bulbocastanum, Onobrychis viciæformis, Centauria solstitialis, Cichorium Intybus. Of bluebells — Campanula glomerata, C. Trachelium, C. latifolia, C. rapunculoides, C. rotundifolia, and C. patula; Vaccinium Myrtillus, Calluna vulgaris, Monotropa Hypopitys, Chlora perfoliata, Menyanthes trifoliata, Cuscuta europæa. Of the nightshades— Solanum Dulcamara, S. nigrum, Hyoscyamus niger. Digitalis purpurea, Linaria repens, Lathrea squamaria, Borago officinalis, Aristolochia Clematitis, Daphne Laureola. In ponds and streams, Thalictrum flavum, Typha latifolia, Sparganium ramosum, Lemna polyrhiza, Sagittaria sagittifolia, Alisma Plantago, Butomus umbellatus.

Of ferns — Lomaria Spicant, Asplenium Adiantum-nigrum, Scolopendrium vulgare, Aspidium aculeatum, A. Trichomanes Nephrodium Filix-mas, Ophioglossum vulgatum, Lastrea spinulosa, L. ulignosa.

Village folk stiil use decoctions of wild and garden plants as medicine or for ointment. Amongst these are rosemary, red sage, balm, peppermint, hyssop, spurge, horehound, pennyroyal, parsley, houseleek, mallow, ground-ivy, millfoil—said to be a "cure for every disease "— water-betony, agrimony, wild thyme, rue—a horrible thick decoction called "syrup of rue" is given to infants—adder's tongue, soapwort—"smooth side (of leaves) for healing, rough side for drawing "—and celandine.

CHAPTER XVI.

———

Dunstable Occurrences in Chronological Order.

THE following occurrences are taken direct from the Anglo-Saxon Chronicle, the Chronicles of Richard of Wendover, Matthew Paris, Hollingshead, the *Annales Prioratus de Dunstaplia*, and other well-known authorities. Sometimes different authorities record the same event, in a slightly different form. The later occurrences are taken from *Diurnals*, general and local histories, and newspapers.

410   The last of the Romans leave the neighbourhood of where Dunstable now is.

571   The Saxons raid and destroy the Brito-Roman village which stood where Dunstable now is. The Britons call their village Dorcobriv ; the Romans, who cannot pronounce Celtic gutturals, call it Duro-cob-rivæ.

921 } The Danes raid and destroy the Saxon village built on the
991 }   site of Dorcobriv. The Saxons call all places and things by new Saxon names, and by the time of the Danish raid Dorcobriv had received a Saxon name, of which there is no record, but it was probably Dunestaple. There may have been a small wooden Christian church.

1086   The enumerators sent by William the Conqueror find nothing but burnt ruins on the site of the present Dunstable, so do not mention it in Domesday Book.

1110   The Miracle Play of St. Katherine performed at Dunstable. This shows that at this time the place had the fixed name of Dunestaple as well as cottages, a school, and probably a small church.

1123   Henry I. at Dunstable, according to Roger of Wendover. It was in this year that the king probably noted the bad roads and the lower grounds and hill-tops covered with bush, and heard of the place being infested with "robbers and beasts.''

1132 Priory of Augustinian Canons founded at Dunstable, in honour of St. Peter, and its first charter granted by Henry I. The king spends his Christmas at Dunstable and invites his subjects to live near his residence there.

1137 Stephen at Dunstable.

1145 Benedictine nunnery, in honour of the Holy Trinity, founded at Markyate Street.

1154 Stephen and Henry, Duke of Normandy, at Dunstable.

1164 Burgesses of Dunstable directed by Henry II. to send representatives to Parliament at Clarendon, in Wiltshire. The summons not obeyed.

1178 Apparition of St. Alban disturbed by Dunstable traders, according to Matthew Paris.

1203 John restores the lordship of Houghton Regis to the Priory, and grants a three days' fair in May in honour of St. Frehemund.

1204 John gives, by his Charter, his house and garden to Dunstable.

1206 The priors again lose their lands at Houghton.

1212 The priors get King John's writ for the recovery of lands at Houghton.
Three persons arrive from the pope to preach a crusade.

1213 Dunstable burnt by accident.
The church dedicated by Hugh II., Bishop of Lincoln.

1214 Stephen, Archbishop of Canterbury, at Dunstable.

1215 John passes a night at Dunstable on his journey to the north.
The barons, under the Earl of Perche, passing through Dunstable, spare neither churches or windows.

1217 Itinerant justices come to Dunstable and take the people's oath of allegiance to Henry III.
Lewis the Dauphin, with the English barons, in arms against the king, halt for a night at Dunstable, after the defeat at Lincoln, and do great damage to the church.

1220 Robert, Bishop of Lismore, at Dunstable.
Hugh, Bishop of Lincoln, at Dunstable.

1221 Mossy, son of Brun, a jew, sues the prior for £700. Mossy's friends pay the king a marc of gold, and afterwards £100, to save the jew from hanging for forgery.

1224 At the siege of Bedford Castle, occupied by Falcasius de Brent, the people of Dunstable, storming the outer bail, get for their share a great number of horses, with harness, arms, and engines, live cattle, hogs and pigs, and a number of houses filled with hay and corn.

1227 The Priory obtains a confirmation of the charters of Henry I. and Richard I.

1229 Henry III., passing through Dunstable, lodges at the Priory. The townsmen forsake the church, become active resisters, and declare they will sooner " go to hell—" infernum descendere "—than submit to be taxed.

1232 Tournament at Dunstable.

1244 A great number of discontented barons and knights assemble at Dunstable and Luton, under pretence of holding a tournament. The tournament prohibited by the king.

1247 Henry III,, with his queen, Prince Edward and Princess Margaret, at Dunstable. The king and queen offer eight silk cloths, and the queen 100s. in silver, for a thurible and pyx. The Priory, in return, give a gilt cup each to the king and queen, and a gold buckle each to Edward and Margaret. The king orders the squatters on local waste lands to be dislodged.

A tournament between Richard, Earl of Gloucester, and Guy de Lusignan prohibited by the king, the latter fearing that " his brother and followers would be cut to pieces."

1249 Bishop of Lincoln at Dunstable.

A general chapter of Augustinians held.

1250 Bishop of Lincoln at Dunstable.

1254 A cup of silver gilt worth 100s. sent to the king.

A tournament prohibited at Dunstable.

1256 A tournament prohibited at Dunstable.

1258 Boniface, Archbishop of Canterbury, at Dunstable.

1259 Brother Ralph, of Studham, slain " in defence of the rights of the church " by the men of the prior of Grovebury.

House of Friars Preachers established at Dunstable, on the south-west of the town.

1263 Simon de Montfort, Earl of Leicester, whilst at Dunstable becomes a brother of the Priory,

1264 Prince Edward ravages the country, whereon the wapentake of Wirkeswyrthe, to save themselves, offer him £200, and lay £10 on the Priory.

Rogues steal sheep near Sewell, and drive them towards Leighton ; two of the thieves are caught, tried, and hanged next day on the top of Pascombe Pit.

Tournament at Dunstable forbidden by the king

1265 King Henry III., his queen, and legate, and Simon de Montfort, at Dunstable.

Tournament prohibited at Dunstable.

Soldiers despoil the nunnery at Flamstead and maltreat the nuns.

1266 Henry III. and Richard, King of Germany, at Dunstable.

1267 Two Welshmen beheaded at Dunstable for robbery.

1272 Four marks paid by the Priory for Prince Edward's crusade in the Holy Land.

A blind man taken into the Priory " for his soul."

1274 Eudo la Suche throws down the priors' gallows at Edessuthe (Blows Downs, towards Caddington Lane), and sets up a gallows below Pudele, which was not there before (now " Gibbet Arch," beyond Puddle Hill). (*See Map*.)

After the death of Prior Simon, all his horses die, and " misfortunes come thick " upon the Priory.

1275 Henry, a converted jew, obtains the pope's letters that the priors maintain him and his family. The official of Lincoln " provides for him elsewhere."

1275 Five thieves hanged, a sixth turns evidence, and hangs
   thirteen more.
  The king and queen lodge with the priors, and the king
   gives one " rich bandekyne," or valuable cloth,
  Richard, Bishop of Lincoln, at Dunstable.

1276 King Edward I. at Dunstable.

1277 A large room began for Edward I, next to the Prior's
   chamber.
  The Archbishop of Canterbury at Dunstable for five days.

1279 A tournament at Dunstable.

1280 Two other tournaments at Dunstable.

1283 Oliver, Bishop of Lincoln, at Dunstable.
  The Prior dines with John Durrant, who makes a feast ; the
   Prior owes John Durrant " much money, so he dares not
   offend him."

1284 Bishop Oliver Sutton at Dunstable.
  John, Archbishop of Canterbury, at Dunstable.

1286 Dunstable causes only to be tried at Dunstable.

1287 Bishop Oliver Sutton at Dunstable

1288 General chapter of Augustinians at Dunstable.
  Bishop Oliver Sutton at Dunstable.

1289 Tournament at Dunstable.

1290 Queen Eleanor dies; her body passes here, and rests for
   one night.
  Two friar preachers of Dunstable celebrate Christmas Day
   at Hertford Castle ; going to bed in good health and
   spirits, are found dead in their beds, "supposed to have
   died suddenly " (!)

1292 Tournament at Dunstable.
  The prior and his servant ferret rabbits in Buckwood stubbs,
   as his common, no'withstanding the complaints made by
   the servants of the lady of Eaton Bray manor.

1293 Tournament at Dunstable.
  The great cross in the church, with the images of St. Mary
   and St. John, new painted, and many other figures of
   saints " new done."

1294 The pope's nuncio at Dunstable.
  In July, search is made by order of King Edward I., after
   wealth laid up by monasteries, cathedrals, and other
   churches. The Priory is searched, but, though they
   searched all the secret places, they only found £40. This
   belonged to Walter Rudham, and was afterwards
   returned.
  Bishop Oliver Sutton at Dunstable.
  Archbishop Winchelsea at the Priory.

1295 Dunstable sends two members to Parliament, until 1338.
   Gaol rebuilt.

1311 Queen Eleanor's Cross erected at Dunstable.

1312 Tournament prohibited at Dunstable.

1319 Tournament prohibited at Dunstable.

1341 King Edward III. and Queen Philippa present at a grand tournament, in commemoration of a great naval victory of the English over the French at Sluys. on the Flemish coast. This is the last date of a tournament, and it will be noted how many such gatherings were prohibited by the reigning kings. Robbery, murder, and rebellion were often associated with tournaments at Dunstable. The Dunstable tournaments took place either in the flat fields at the base of Blows Downs, near the Luton road, or in the flat fields near Bullpond Lane—the old "Butts."

1349 In the plague, the townsmen make themselves a bell, and call it "Mary."

1375 Confirmation of the liberties of the Priory by Edward III.

1381 Dunstable attacked by a rebellious mob, who extort a charter from the prior, which is afterwards revoked.

1390 (about) John of Dunstable, a world-famous musician and mathematician, born.

1414 William Murlie, a Dunstable brewer and Lollard, hanged at Harringay, near London.

1457 Henry VI and Queen Margaret at Dunstable.

1458 John of Dunstable, musician, dies and is buried at Luton.

1459 Henry VI. at Dunstable ; proclamation to the townsmen.

1533 Queen Katherine, residing at Ampthill, is cited by Cranmer, Archbishop of Canterbury, to appear at Dunstable. Divorce read in the queen's absence, in the Lady Chapel of the Priory, on July 25th. The divorce is probably also read publicly to the people from the recently removed external gallery of the west front of the church, and a copy of the words of the divorce fixed to one of the western doors.

1536 Death of Katherine, at Kimbolton, Huntingdonshire,

1539 Dissolution of the Priory of Dunstable and Abbey of Woburn.
Robert Hobbs, the last abbot of the latter, hanged.

1540 Henry VIII. at Dunstable. It is reported—Willis's " Mitred Abbeys "—that he wished to make Dunstable a cathedral city.

1541 Henry VIII. again at Dunstable.

1552 Edward VI. grants the rectory and advowson of Dunstable to the dean and canons of Windsor.

1569 A primitive fire-engine made.

1572 Elizabeth at Dunstable

1603 Cholera very fatal at Dunstable.

1607 The last county assizes held at Dunstable.

1625 Cholera very fatal at Dunstable.

1638 Daniel Fossey's halfpenny token struck.

1643 Eleanor cross demolished.

1644 Charles I. sends a party of soldiers to Dunstable, who plunder the town and commit great outrages in the church during divine service, shooting at the minister in the pulpit and wounding several of the congregation.

1645   Charles, with his army on their way to Naseby, arrived at
         Dunstable.   The king sleeps at the " Red Lion " inn.
1648   Elkanah Settle, city poet, born.
1654   Intention of marriage betwixt Thomas Wats and Jane Long,
         both of Dunstable, " published in the Market."
1661   Cholera very fatal at Dunstable.
1664   William Strange leaves by will . £10 for the poor of the
         parish, but none to be given to " quakers or common
         beggars."   Dunstable was the meeting-place of quakers
         from neighbouring towns till 1799,
1667   William Chew's halfpenny token struck.
1668   Daniel Finche's halfpenny token struck.
1708   Followers of John Bunyan establish themselves in St.
         Mary's Street, Dunstable, this being the great rallying
         place for Baptists for twelve miles round.
1717   " Sugar-loaf " hotel built.
1723   The sisters Cart and Ashton present the picture (now des-
         troyed) to the church representing the Last Supper, similar
         to that in St. George's Chapel, Windsor Castle, painted
         by Sir James Thornhill.
1742   The first coach runs through Dunstable from London to
         Litchfield ; three days were occupied in the journey.
1770   Urn full of Roman coins of Antoninus and Constantine
         found near Whipsnade turning on Dunstable Downs.
1773   The manor leased to the Duke of Bedford for three lives.
         Some followers of John Bunyan leave Bedford for
         Kensworth.
1776   Eight ancient bells taken from the Church belfry and
         recast.
1777   The Rev. Dr. William Dodd, vicar of Hockliffe, hanged for
         forgery.
1781   Dunstable Church robbed.
1782   A new coach road is made on the west side of Chalk Hill, in
         the valley, as marked on map—not over the hill—costs
         £16,000.
1784   Road made from Dunstable to Luton ; it previously ran
         from Dunstable to Leagrave.   Road made from Oxford,
         through Dunstable to Cambridge.
1790   A second Baptist chapel built.
1793   Nanny Burton dies, a very old woman, who established and
         taught in the first Sunday School in Dunstable—a school
         which is said to have been the second Sunday School in
         England.
         A coarse, mock play bill published regarding a suppositious
         entertainment at a mythical theatre by a non-existant
         " Sylvester Daggerwood."   *Sylvester Daggerwood* is one of
         George Colman's plays, not a person.
1798   The great enclosures of land.
1801   The first squatter encroachment by building on waste land
         in Church Street.   Population, 1,296 ; houses, 243.
1802   Money left to establish the first church Sunday School in
         Dunstable.

1803 The gibbet at " Gib Arch," beyond Puddle Hill, destroyed.
Houses in Middle Row pulled down opposite the " Red Lion " hotel ; site of the Eleanor cross discovered.

1805 Old Market house removed from middle of street, and rebuilt on site of present Town Hall.

1807 The Bunyan meeting-house, or Old Baptists' chapel, in St. Mary's Street, enlarged and a Sunday School founded.

1809 A prize-fight suppressed on Dunstable Downs by 120 volunteers.

1811 A row of beech-trees in Churchyard cut down ; beneath the roots large numbers of human bones found.

1812 Wesleyan Methodists first appear in the town.

1814 Further building encroachments on waste land in Church Street.
William Gutteridge finds a Palæolithic implement near Caddington, and preserves it as something unusual, 17 years before the first European discoveries are published in France.

1831 The first Wesleyan Methodist chapel built.

1835 The site of the Friars Preechers' buildings excavated, and examined in Spittle Close, opposite the " Half Moon " inn, and on the north side of Half Moon Lane. Forty feet of wall, two and a-half feet high, is found ; the base of a round column two feet in diameter ; stones of a semi-circular arch ; window tracery, painted glass, tiles, and two coffins—one of stone and one of lead—containing skeletons.
Dunstable General Provident Institution founded.

1836 Dunstable " workhouse "—a comfortless and dilapidated structure of fourteen rooms, on the north side of the " Swan " inn, High Street South—abolished, and the paupers, forty-two in number, removed to the Union House at Luton,

1837 Chalk hill-cutting made ; cost, £10,000.
A man accidentally killed by a bell in the church belfry.
Gas introduced in Dunstable. Previous to this date the town was lighted by lanterns, candles, and oil-lamps.

1838 Regular stage-coaches ceased running through the town on the opening of the London and Birmingham railway.

1839 Church-Sunday and Day-Schools erected on south side of Church Street, on the site of a former weekly plant market.
The manor reverts from the Dukes of Bedford to the Crown

1841 Victoria and Albert pass through Dunstable on their way to Woburn.
Great fire in High Street and Church Street ; nineteen houses destroyed.

1843 Dunstable made a Wesleyan circuit, with local preachers.
" Bible-Schools " opened.

1844 Large fire, in which the Wesleyan Chapel and adjoining farm buildings are destroyed.
Beating the bounds by Free-School boys discontinued.

N

1845   Wesleyan Chapel rebuilt ; cost, £2,000.

George Stephenson offers, by a Luton, Dunstable, St. Albans, and Watford railway, to " reinstate Dunstable in its former position as an important town on the Great Northern thoroughfare ; " he had visited Luton with the expectation of being kindly received in offering to carry out the extension line ; but, having met with anything but kindness, had resolved never to revisit them as long as he lived, unless for other purposes."

1845-1850   Nineteen portions of waste land leased to Dunstable residents.

1847   The present Baptist chapel built in West Street, at a cost of £2,100.

1848   Railway between Dunstable and Leighton Buzzard opened.

1849   The Bunyan meeting-house injured by the fall of its roof ; a new chapel erected, at a cost of £500.

1850   Tumulus opened on Dunstable Downs, by Bedfordshire Archæological Society.

1851   Restoration of Priory Church, commenced in August.

1852   Restoration of South Aisle of Church.

1853   Wesleyan Day School opened.

1854   Primitive Methodist Chapel built ; cost, £1,400.

1855   First local newspaper published—*Dunstable Chronicle*.
A savings bank established at the Town Hall.

1858   Railway from Dunstable to Luton opened.

1859   Dunstable Volunteer Corps established.

1861   Cemetery opened ; cost, £3,000.

1863   Telegraph posts erected through the town.
Local Board instituted.

1864   Charter of Victoria granted.

1865   First municipal election.
Borough police established.

1866   Commission of Peace issued.
Old Town Hall purchased by the Corporation.

1869   Clock Tower erected on Town Hall.

1870   Market tolls and Crown land purchased by Corporation.

1872   Corn exchange opened.
Church restoration, £10,000.

1873   Waterworks opened.

1875   Trees planted in streets.

1877   Volunteer Review in valley at foot of Dunstable Downs.

1879   Town hall destroyed by fire.

1880   Town Hall rebuilt.

1886   The 1569 fire-engine sold to Messrs. Shand & Mason, of London.

1888   Grammar School opened.
Totternhoe land enclosures.

1892   Brewers' Hill Road opened.

1894   Trees planted on Dunstable Downs.

1901-1902   Drainage of Dunstable completed.

1903   Worthington George Smith made first freeman of the borough.

1904   Robbery of plate from the Church.

BENE VALE.

" Don'ts " for Picnic Parties.

The Council of the Selborne Society urgently requests visitors to treat the country they are visiting with the reverence due to natural beauty.

DON'T gather such quantities of wild flowers and ferns that before the day is over you are obliged to throw them away on the roadside. By such gathering you injure the flora of the district, and you take away pleasures from many people who like to see flowers and ferns growing in their native haunts.

DON'T disturb the birds in their breeding season.

DON'T litter the places visited with waste papers or torn letters.

DON'T leave empty bottles and other débris of your picnic to vulgarise the spots, the scenery of which you have been enjoying.

INDEX.

DUNSTABLE AND ITS NEIGHBOURHOOD, Showing Old and New Roads, Lanes, Public Footways and Antiquities

MAP OF DUNSTABLE & NEIGHBOURHOOD
SHOWING OLD & NEW ROADS, LANES, PUBLIC FOOTWAYS & ANTIQUITIES

SCALE OF 1   3/4   1/2   1/4   1 MILE   2 MILES

Scale of 2½ inches to the Statute Mile.

Drawn and Copyrighted by the Author.

DATE OF GREAT ENCLOSURES 1798

Place names and labels:

DUNSTABLE
DUNE-STAPEL
HOUGHTON REGIS — HOCTONE — HOUSTONE (DOMESDAY)
TILSWORTH — TULLESWORTH (NOR. FR. INS. IN CH.)
STANBRIDGE — STANBURGE (DOMESDAY)
SEWELL — SEWELLE (DOMESDAY)
TOTTERNHOE — TOTTENEHOU — TOTTENHOU (DOMESDAY)
EATON BRAY — ETONE — EITONE (DOMESDAY)
EDLESBOROUGH — EDINGEBERGE (DOMESDAY)
KENSWORTH — CANESWORDE (DOMESDAY)
CADDINGTON — CADENDONE (DOMESDAY)
LEAGRAVE
PILEWORDE (DOMESDAY)
LYC-EANBIRG — ANC-SAX-CHRON. A.D. 795.
SOURCE OF LEA
RIVER LEA
LEWSEY HILL
PUDDLE HILL
GREEN MAN
BIDWELL — BIDWELL FARM — ST. BRIGID'S OR BRIDE'S WELL
ARDLEY HILL
STRIPER'S HILL
MOUNT PLEASANT
COXEN HILL
WEST FIELD
LANCOT HILL
COLD HARBOUR
DO-LITTLE MILL — DOLE
ICKNIELD WAY
DUNSTABLE WAY
WATLING STREET ROMAN ROAD
OLD COACH ROAD 1782
ROMAN ROAD B
LEIGHTON BUZZARD AND DUNSTABLE RAILWAY
LEIGHTON BUZZARD, DUNSTABLE & LUTON RAILWAY
STANBRIDGE FORD STATION
DUNSTABLE PARK
ISOLATION HOSPITAL
TUMULUS No. 6 WITH ROMAN & CHILD
TUMULUS No. 7
NEOLITHS
CELT
DURO-COBIS / DUROCOBRIVIS
MAP OF DUNSTABLE & NEIGHBOURHOOD
Worthington G. Smith 1904.
To HOCKLIFFE
To TODDINGTON
To CHALTON
To SUNDON
To LUTON
To MARKYATE
To IVINGHOE
To DAGNALL
To STANBRIDGE
To LIMBURY
To KINSBURY
WOODSIDE

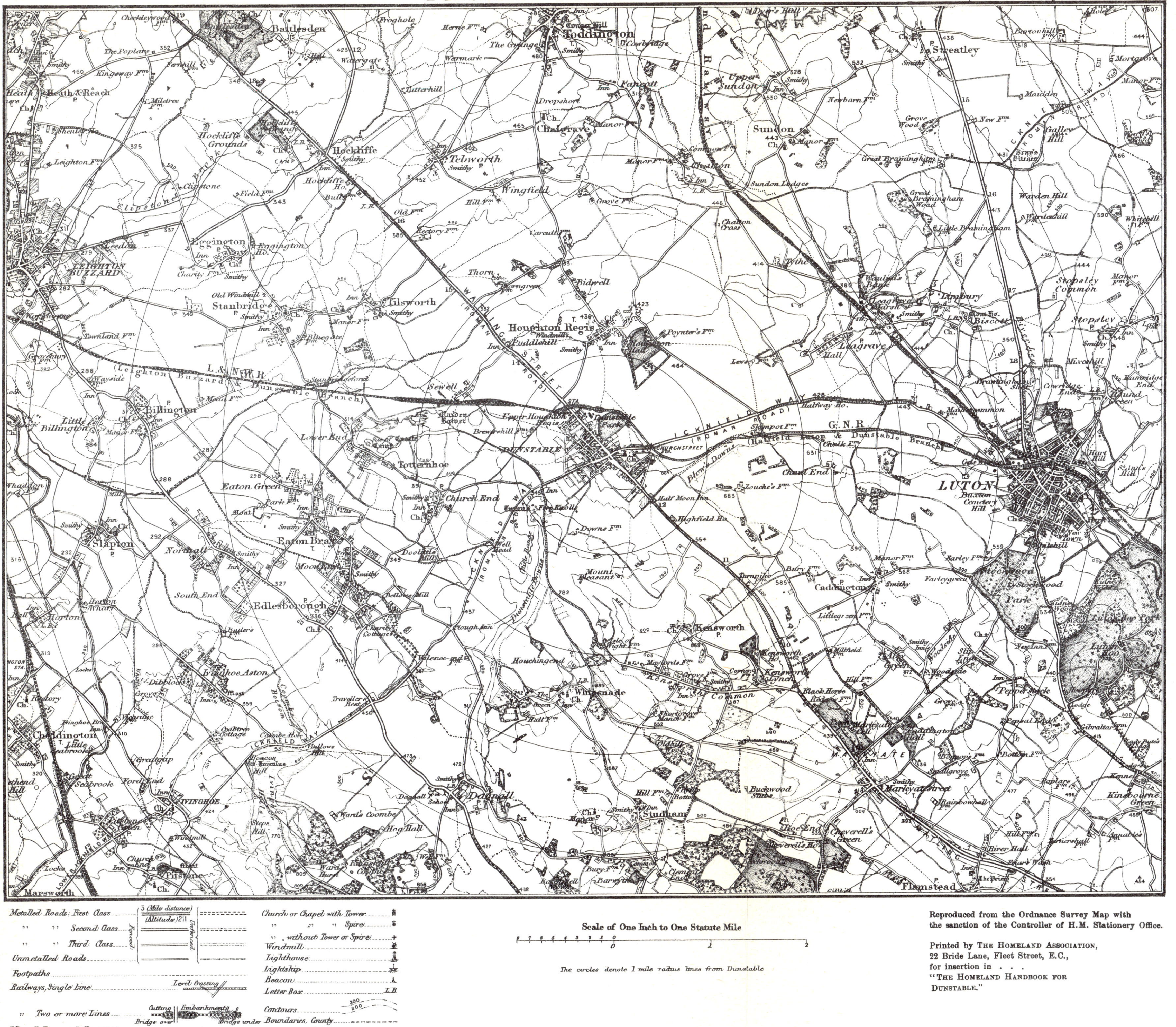

DUNSTABLE WITH ITS SURROUNDINGS.

Metalled Roads, First Class
" " Second Class
" " Third Class
Unmetalled Roads
Footpaths
Railways, Single Line
" Two or more Lines
Mineral Lines and Tramways
Rivers and Streams when exceeding 15 feet in width are shown with two lines.
For other information see Characteristic Sheet.

3 (Mile distance)
(Altitude) 211
Level Crossing
Cutting   Embankment
Bridge over   Bridge under

Church or Chapel with Tower
" " Spire
" without Tower or Spire
Windmill
Lighthouse
Lightship
Beacon
Letter Box   L.B.
Contours
Boundaries, County
" Parish

Scale of One Inch to One Statute Mile
The circles denote 1 mile radius lines from Dunstable.

Reproduced from the Ordnance Survey Map with
the sanction of the Controller of H.M. Stationery Office.

Printed by THE HOMELAND ASSOCIATION,
22 Bride Lane, Fleet Street, E.C.,
for insertion in . . .
"THE HOMELAND HANDBOOK FOR
DUNSTABLE."

FOR REGISTER

OF ALL THE AVAILABLE

PROPERTIES

TO BE LET OR SOLD IN

Dunstable & District,

. . APPLY TO . .

John Homan Thorpe,

Auctioneer, Valuer,

Land and Estate Agent,

76, High Street,

DUNSTABLE, Beds.

National Telephone No. 041.

Where to Stay at Dunstable.

THE SARACEN'S HEAD HOTEL,

HIGH STREET SOUTH.

Old Established Family and Commercial.

MOTOR AND CYCLE HOUSE.

FREDK. R. HATCHER, *Proprietor.*

GARAGE.

Pratt's or Bowley's Spirit, Carless Capel's Petrol,
Carburine, Lubricating Oils, Grease, Carbide, &c.

Pit for Repairs.

Telegrams: "SARACEN'S, DUNSTABLE."
Midland Railway Company's Parcel Receiving Office.

DUNSTABLE SCHOOL.

Ashton Grammar School.

EDUCATION FOR THE UNIVERSITIES.

SCHOLARSHIPS GAINED—Army, Navy, Civil Service, Medical and Law Schools, Engineering, etc.

Special Classes also given in Shorthand, Book-keeping, etc.

TERMS (for Day Boys): £7 10s. od. per Annum.

THE SCHOOL HOUSE

Under the personal care of the Headmaster, has accommodation for 53 Boarders.

**TERMS (inclusive of Board and Tuition):
£50 os. od. per Annum.**

ASHTON LODGE

Is a School Boarding House, adjoining the School Premises, under the charge of E. E. APTHORP, ESQ., B.A. Here each Boy has a separate Bedroom.

**TERMS (inclusive of Board and Tuition):
£60 per Annum.**

SPECIAL CARRIAGES ARE RESERVED

By the Railway Authorities for Boys coming from and returning to Luton, and the School Sergeant travels to and fro with them.

THE SCHOOL GROUNDS and PLAYING FIELDS ARE UPWARDS OF THIRTEEN ACRES IN EXTENT, the Cricket and Football Ground being in the healthiest and highest part of the Town. Here the County Cricket Club play some of their Matches.

THE BUILDINGS INCLUDE—

A Swimming Bath, lined with White Glazed Tiles, 80-ft. by 30-ft.

A Fives-Court of the Rugby Pattern.

A Gymnasium, 40-ft. by 28-ft., fitted with all necessary Appliances.

A Chemical Laboratory fully fitted for Practical Work.

A Carpenter's Shop with all necessary Appliances.

The whole School is regularly drilled in Military and Physical Drill, and all Boys who are old enough are taught to shoot at the Morris Tube Range.

Golf Links have been laid out in the Park, for the use of the School only, within three minutes walk of the School. Golf is only permitted in the Winter Terms, and is chiefly for Boys who, for any reason, are unable to play Football or Hockey.

Prospectus and full Particulars may be obtained from the Headmaster—

L. C. R. THRING, M.A.

Dunstable School House from the North.

Part of Dunstable School Cricket Field during a Match.

DAY AND BOARDING SCHOOL FOR GIRLS.

WENTWORTH HOUSE,

DUNSTABLE.

Principal - - **MISS BEAMAN**

(B.A. Honours, London.　Registered by Teachers' Registration Council).

TERMS MODERATE AND INCLUSIVE.

Pupils prepared successfully for Cambridge Local and other Examinations.

A limited number of Boarders can be taken, and receive every care and attention.　A considerable reduction is made in the case of Weekly Boarders.　Reductions also for daughters of Clergymen and for sisters.

Prospectus and all Particulars on application.

Reference kindly permitted to—

L. C. R. THRING, Esq.,
　　Head Master of the Boys' Grammar School, Dunstable.

LT.-COLONEL FORMAN and MRS. FORMAN,
　　　　　　　　　　　　Bombay, India.

DR. and MRS. WILLEY,
　　Laurel Road, Leicester.

MRS. PEARSON,
　　43, Queen's Gardens,
　　　　Lancaster Gate, W.　Etc., Etc.

Arthur W. Nash,

Builder and General

Contractor. 

SPECIAL ATTENTION GIVEN TO

ALTERATIONS AND GENERAL REPAIRS.

Sanitary Work a Speciality.

ESTIMATES SUBMITTED AND SANITARY
SURVEYS MADE FREE OF CHARGE.

ADDRESS: 

PRINCESS STREET, DUNSTABLE.

Telephone: 042 DUNSTABLE.
Telegrams: "NASH, DUNSTABLE."

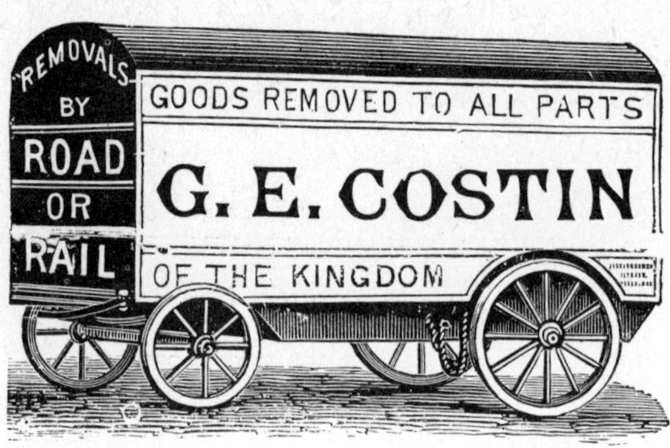
REMOVALS BY ROAD OR RAIL
GOODS REMOVED TO ALL PARTS
G. E. COSTIN
OF THE KINGDOM

RIXSON BROS., The Old Retreat, HIGH STREET, DUNSTABLE.

UPHOLSTERERS. CABINET MAKERS. FURNITURE REMOVALS.

The Largest Stock of Genuine Antique Furniture and Works of Art, etc., in the District.

Best Prices Given for Genuine Antiques.

A CORNER.—ANTIQUE SHOWROOM.

Where to Shop at Dunstable.

MILES TAYLOR,

Printer and Stationer,

"*Gazette*" Office, DUNSTABLE.

LETTERPRESS PRINTING of every description, with neatness and despatch, and at reasonable charges.

STATIONERY AND FANCY DEPOT

Picture Post Cards and Views of the Neighbourhood a Speciality.

Circulating Library in connection with Mudie's.

ESTABLISHED 1887.

R. FORREST, DUNSTABLE,
(late LEVITT),

Toy, Stationery and Fancy Goods Dealer, and Wholesale and Retail Tobacconist.

A Large Stock of Well=Seasoned British and Foreign Cigars.

Cigarettes and Tobaccos by all the Leading Makers. Walking Sticks, Pipes, Pouches, &c., &c.

Novelties in Fancy Goods arriving Daily.

Cheapest House in the Trade for Stationery and Pictorial Postcards.

DOLLS A SPECIALITY.

Where to Shop at Dunstable.

VICTORIA BUN HOUSE.

JOSEPH ANDREWS (Late Shepherd,)

Wholesale and Retail Pastrycook, Confectioner and Caterer,

10, High Street, Dunstable.

Raised Pork Pies, Pastry and Cakes, fresh daily, and to order. Rich Madeira, Dundee, Mould, Dessert, and Luncheon Cakes, always in Stock.

WEDDING CAKES, a Speciality (Diploma of Merit, Awarded at Bakers' and Confectioners' Exhibition, Agricultural Hall, London, September, 1903), **from 1/6 per lb., exquisitely decorated, and carefully packed, distance no object.**

Silver Stands, and Cutlery let on Hire, at Moderate Charges.

Wedding Receptions, & Ball Suppers provided, School Treats, and Band of Hope parties liberally catered for, estimates given.

Suitable for Presents, etc.—A Large Assortment of all the Latest Season's Novelties, in Fancy Boxes of Chocolates, Biscuits, Sweets, etc., from all the leading Manufacturers.

Game Pies, Plum Puddings, Christmas Cakes, etc., to order.

Orders by Wire or Post carefully and promptly attended to.

All Goods are manufactured from the finest and best ingredients only.

A Trial and Recommendations are respectfully solicited.

Where to Shop at Dunstable.

Telephone No. 0636.

S. FARMER & Co.'s
Pianos and Organs

BY THE

GREAT MAKERS,

At the Lowest Cash Prices or on Easy Terms.

HIGH-CLASS TUNING A SPECIALITY.

3, WEST STREET, DUNSTABLE,

And at LUTON.

ESTABLISHED 1881.

REMEMBER!

The 'Traveller' Cycle
. and Motor Works,

HIGH STREET, DUNSTABLE,

Is the OLDEST and BEST place in THE NEIGH-
. BOURHOOD for everything connected with
. WHEELING. . . .

Special and Prompt Attention given to all kinds of REPAIRS.

PRICES ALWAYS REASONABLE.

W. SCOTT, Proprietor.   Official Repairer to the
                                                C.T.C.

THIS BOOK 

may be taken as a

Sample of

Printing

. executed by .

GIBBS & BAMFORTH,

Limited,

Fine Art, General, and

Catalogue Printers,

Dagnall Street,

ST. ALBANS.

Telephone—No. 62 St. Albans.

ILLUSTRATIONS 

APPEAL to every one. The child before it can read is attracted by the picture book, before it can write it attempts to convey its thoughts by means of pictures (which are only worthy of that name in the opinion of the parents), in later years the illustrations in the periodicals generally receive first attention, while the recent development of picture postcards is further demonstration of the same principle. Therefore we think that an advertisement emanating from a firm whose business is the making of illustrations will not be out of place in a publication such as this. We cater mostly for Printers and Publishers, but are happy to place our services at the disposal of any one who requires reproductions of drawings, photos, and pictures.

Our Departments

Two and Three-colour, Half-tone, Line, Wood, and Steel Plate Engravings. Poster and Advertisement Designing. Drawing. ◎ ◎ Touching up Photographs. ◎ Clay Modelling. ◎ ◎ ◎ ◎ ◎

THE "ARC" ENGRAVING CO., LTD.

STUDIOS AND OFFICES : **4 & 6, FARRINGDON AVENUE, LONDON, E.C.**

ST. BRIDE'S PRESS PUBLICATIONS.

Public Works.

15th of every Month.
Yearly, 16s. (post free).

Authoritative Monographs on Engineering Works in all Parts of the World.

The Surveyor and Municipal and County Engineer.

Every Friday, 3d.
Yearly, 15s. (post free).

For Municipal and County Engineers, Consulting Engineers, Contractors and Members of Local Authorities.

TECHNICAL PUBLICATIONS.

(Send Post Card for Complete List.)

10. **Drainage Works and Sanitary Fittings.** By WILLIAM H. MAXWELL, A.M.I.C.E. *Second Edition.* Price 1s., post free.

13. **The Sewerage Engineer's Note Book,** being Standard Notes on Sewer Formulæ and Sewerage Calculations. By ALBERT WOLLHEIM, A.M.I.C.E. *Second (Revised) Edition.* Price 3s. 6d., post free.

22. **Diagrams Exhibiting the Discharges and Velocities of Circular and Oval Sewers and Water Conduits, together with Notes on the Design of Sewerage Schemes.** By EDWIN B. NEWTON, F.S.I., A.M.I.C.E., &c. Price 2s 6d, post free.

23. **The Construction of Roads and Streets,** with Historical Sketch of the Art of Road-making ; and numerous specially-prepared illustrations. By WM. H. MAXWELL, A.M.I.C.E. Price 3s. 6d., post free.

ST. BRIDE'S PRESS PUBLICATIONS.

LONDON : The St. Bride's Press, Ltd., 22 & 24, Bride Lane, and 3, 4 & 13, New Street Hill, Fleet Street, E.C.

Councils and Education Press Publications.

Education—Primary, Secondary and Technical.

Every Thursday, Price 3d.

Yearly, 12s. (6/6 to Members of the Teaching Profession.)

The Official Educational Organ of the County Councils' Association, the Association of Directors and Secretaries for Education, the Association of Technical Institutions, and the Association of Teachers of Domestic Science.

The County Council Times.

Every Wednesday, 3d.
Yearly, 12s. (post free).

The Official Organ of the County Councils of the United Kingdom.

LONDON : The Councils and Education Press, Ltd., 24, Bride Lane, Fleet Street, EC.

HERBERT A. STRANGE,

23, High Street, Dunstable,

Photographic Artist,

And Dealer in Photographic Materials.

**Children's
Portraits
a Speciality.**

**Enlargements
of every
Description.**

**Flashlight
Photos of
Evening
Parties.**

**Personal
Attention
given to
Groups.**

**Photos by
Day or Night.**

**The Largest
Selection of
Local Views
in the District**

CAMERAS and ACCESSORIES,

AND EVERYTHING FOR THE AMATEUR.

**ENGRAVINGS.
PHOTOGRAVURES.
CHROMOS.**

**PICTURE FRAMES.
ALUMINIUM
NOVELTIES.**

Where to Shop at Dunstable.

KILBY & SONS,

Fancy Bread & Biscuit Bakers,

Pastry Cooks & Confectioners,

72, HIGH STREET NORTH & 34, EDWARD STREET

DUNSTABLE.

GOOD ACCOMMODATION FOR CYCLISTS.

FAMILIES WAITED UPON DAILY.

OUR SPECIALITIES.

Hovis, Bermeline, Artox, Vienna and all kinds of Fancy Bread.   Fresh Daily.

BRIDE & BIRTHDAY CAKES.

Orders for Picnics & School Treats Promptly Attended to.

AGENTS FOR HOVIS FOODS & BISCUITS.

TEAS & LIGHT REFRESHMENTS.

Winners of Gold and Bronze Medals for Bread in
Competitions open to the United Kingdom.

G. J. TENNANT

. FOR . *Watches, Clocks, Jewellery,*

Silver, and Electro Plate.

A LARGE AND WELL-SELECTED STOCK.

Repairing Department.

G. J. T. is thoroughly competent to undertake every class of Repairs, including Repeaters, Chronometers, &c., having had four years experience in the Largest Watch Repairing Firm in the United Kingdom.

NOTE ADDRESS:

MANCHESTER STREET, Opposite Cattle Market, LUTON.

AND AT DUNSTABLE.

Where to Shop at Dunstable.

HENRY LIMBREY,

(Successor to the Late J. H. LIMBREY),

West Street, DUNSTABLE,

GENERAL IRONMONGER AND COPPERSMITH,

Gas, Water, and Steam Fitter, Metal Worker, &c.

Sanitary and Bath Work.

All Kinds of Pumps Fixed and Repaired.

COOKING AND HEATING APPLIANCES.

RANGE FITTING AND GENERAL REPAIRS.

Mantel Registers, Mantelpieces in Marble, Slate and Wood.

Cutlery and Plate.

W. A. STIMSON,

53, George Street, LUTON,

Tailor & Breeches Maker

Sporting and Military Outfitters.

Outfits for Preparatory and Public Schools.

LADIES' TAILOR & HABIT MAKER.

Patterns, Illustrations, Quotations, Measure Forms sent per return post free on application. . . . .

A Representative will attend Customers at their own residences when desired.

LIST OF BRANCHES—

SHREWSBURY	37, High Street.
LUDLOW	16 & 17, High Street.
ALCESTER	Evesham Street.
DULVERTON, Somerset	Fore Street.
WORCESTER	60, Foregate Street.
JOHANNESBURG	P.O.B. 1682, Barnato Buildings.
LONDON	9, Hanover Square, W.

Where to Shop at Dunstable.

GO TO—   **F. MONK,**

For the Newest Styles in Dress Materials,
6¾d. to 3/11½.

Don't forget our Navy and Black FEARNOUGHT SERGES,
8¾d. to 2/11½.

JACKETS & MANTLES in all the Latest Styles, from 4/11 to 29/6.

Moreen and Felt Skirts in all the Latest Styles, from **1/11½ to 8/11.**

For SHEETINGS, CALICOES, FLANNELS & FLANNELETTES
we are unequalled for value.

PRINTS, SATEENS AND MUSLINS in all the Newest Designs,
1¾d. to 6¾d.   See value and compare.

CURTAINS AND CURTAIN NETS in Big Variety.

RIBBONS, LACES, CHIFFONS AND TULES in all the Leading
Colours.

NOTE THE ADDRESS—

F. MONK, 20, High Street, DUNSTABLE.

A. D. SINFIELD,

WHOLESALE AND RETAIL

TOBACCONIST and STATIONER.

Circulating Library and Registry Office for
Servants.

27, High Street South,
and 30, West Street,

DUNSTABLE.

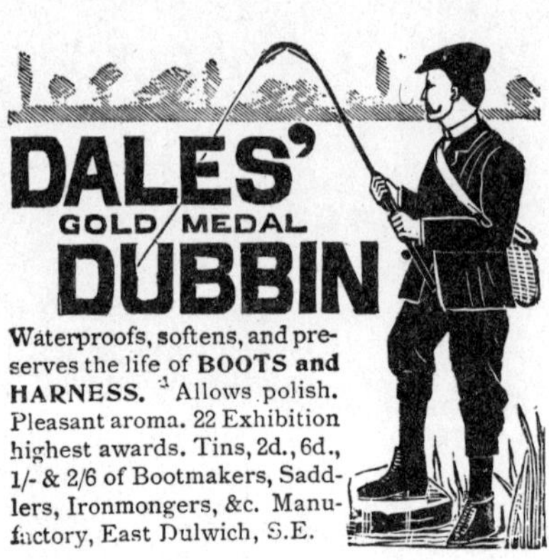

Where to Shop at Dunstable.

CHOICE CUT FLOWERS.

Seed Merchants, Fruiterers,

Greengrocers, &c.

Licensed Dealers

in Game.

15,

High Street, North,

DUNSTABLE, Beds.

FAMILIES WAITED UPON DAILY.

Agent for the Scottish Accident Insurance Company; The London and Lancashire Insurance Company; Employers' Liability Act; and Horse and Carriage Company.

MILLINERY TO SUIT ALL TASTES.

Experience is the best Teacher, and it has taught me to study the Style best suited to my Individual Customers. If you have any doubt give me a trial order and you will not fail to be pleased.

C. E. BIGG, Milliner,

76, HIGH STREET NORTH, DUNSTABLE.

MEAT IS MEAT

But there are many qualities. My business is to supply meat of Prime Quality. At my Shop you can rely upon buying the best quality meat at the lowest possible price. I invite you to prove it by giving me a trial.

ADDRESS :

J. J. HAWKINS, Albion St., Dunstable.

Where to Shop at Dunstable.

THE CONFECTIONERY BAZAAR,

70, HIGH STREET, DUNSTABLE.

High-Class Confectionery and **Fancy Boxes of Chocolates** in great variety by the Best Makers.

J. BOSKETT,

FAMILY GROCER and PROVISION MERCHANT.

High-Class Goods at the Lowest Prices.

Fresh Butter twice a week.   Noted for Dried Fruits, Bacon & Cheese.

43, *HIGH STREET SOUTH, DUNSTABLE.*

W. H. Hutchins, High=class Tailor,

6, CHURCH STREET, DUNSTABLE.

**Newest Styles in LOUNGE, REEFER, NORFOLK, . . .
. MORNING, DRESS & FROCK SUITS. BREECHES
. and GAITERS.   WATERPROOFS, &c.**

Established 1893.

W. M. CLARK, Dunstable, Beds,

TOBACCO BLENDER.

Private Blends a Speciality.

Where to Shop at Dunstable.

VISITORS TO DUNSTABLE

AS well as residents will find it advantageous to pay me a visit. My Store is replete with all kinds of Stationery and Fancy Goods, including View Books, Pictorial Post Cards, Current Literature, and an endless variety of Useful Articles suitable for Presentation. **PRINTING DEPARTMENT**—I have special facilities for doing every kind of Printing with promptitude. Estimates given for all kinds of work.

Address—

J. H. PROVERBS (*Sub Post Office, near the Grammar School,*) DUNSTABLE.

W. H. HUNT,

SADDLER & HARNESS MAKER,

173, HIGH STREET, DUNSTABLE.

Horses fitted on Reasonable Terms.   Ropes and Twines of every description.   Portmanteaus Repaired.

W. BROOKS,

BAKER AND *MEALMAN,*

Upper Union Street, DUNSTABLE.

ALL KINDS OF CAKES MADE TO ORDER.

Families Waited upon Daily.

Established 70 Years.

EDWARD EAMES,

FARRIER, WHITESMITH, &c.,

(NEAR THE POST OFFICE) High Street North, Dunstable.

IMPLEMENTS OF ALL KINDS REPAIRED.

Sole Proprietor of Eames' Celebrated Horse Ointment, which has an unrivalled reputation of 50 years' standing.

Where to Shop at Dunstable.

W. SUMMERFIELD.

Painter, Glazier and Decorator,
Plumber, Gas and Water Fitter.

ESTIMATES GIVEN. **A TRIAL SOLICITED.**

48, *HIGH STREET SOUTH, DUNSTABLE.*

Depot for the Celebrated C.B. Corsets.

W. H. EMERTON,

FANCY DRAPER & GENERAL OUTFITTER,
15, HIGH STREET, DUNSTABLE.

Goods not in Stock procured on the Shortest Notice.
C.B. Corsets from 2/11½ to 21/- per pair.

C. K. BOSKETT,

HAIRDRESSER & PERFUMER,

175, MIDDLE ROW, DUNSTABLE.

ALL KINDS OF TOILET REQUISITES.
LADIES' SHAMPOOING SALOON.
A CHOICE ASSORTMENT OF UMBRELLAS AND WALKING STICKS.

COMMERCIAL AND
TEMPERANCE HOTEL
67, High Street North,
DUNSTABLE.

Moderate Tariff.
**Best Accommodation for Com-
mercials, Cyclists, and the General
Public.**
WILLIAM WRIGHT,
Proprietor.

APARTMENTS.

Visitors to Dunstable will
find suitable Apartments at

GLENDEVON,

Winfield Street,

Dunstable.

THE HOMELAND HANDBOOKS.

No.   CLOTH. PAPER.

1 **Tonbridge for the Angler, the Holiday-Maker and the Resident**
By STANLEY MARTIN and PRESCOTT ROW ... ... 1/- 6d.
2 **Tunbridge Wells of To-Day.** By STANLEY MARTIN and PRESCOTT ROW 1/- 6d.
3 **"London Town."** By ERIC HAMMOND. With Map ... ... 1/- 6d.
4 **"Lyonesse": The Isles of Scilly.** Third Edition. With Introduction by the late SIR WALTER BESANT. Map ... ... 1/- 6d.
5 **"Wolfe-Land": The Westerham District, Kent.** By GIBSON THOMPSON. Third Edition (1903). Ordnance Map 1/6 1/-
6 **"Kent's Capital": Maidstone.** Second Edition. With Map. By STANLEY MARTIN and PRESCOTT ROW ... ... 1/- 6d.
7 **Croydon, New and Old.** Second Edition. With Map. By EDWARD A. MARTIN, F.G.S., and J. E. MORRIS, B.A. ... ... 1/- 6d.
8 **Dartmoor and its Surroundings.** Second Edition. With Map. By BEATRIX F. CRESSWELL ... ... 1/6 6d.
9 **Rochester and Chatham with Pen and Camera.** Second Edition. With Map. By A. G. MUNRO, B.A.... ... ... 1/6 6d.
10 **Reigate and Redhill.** By T. FRANCIS W. HAMILTON. With Map ... 1/- 6d.
11 **"Surrey's Capital": Guildford and District.** Second Edition. With Map. By J. E. MORRIS, B.A. ... ... 1/6 6d.
12 **Dulverton and District: The Country of the Wild Red Deer.** Second Edition. Cloth Edition contains Map. By F. J. SNELL, B.A. 1/6 6d.
13 **Farnham and its Surroundings.** By GORDON HOME. With Introduction by the late EDNA LYALL. With Map 2/- 1/-
14 **Godalming and its Surroundings.** With Map. By T. F. W. HAMILTON ... ... 1/6 6d.
15 **Teignmouth and its Surroundings.** With Map. BY BEATRIX F. CRESSWELL... ... ... 1/6 6d.
16 **Hastings and St. Leonards.** With Plan. By W. H. SANDERS ... 1/6 6d.
17 **Epsom and its Surroundings.** With Map. By GORDON HOME. With a Prefatory Note by "A.R." ... ... 1/6 9d.
18 **Minehead, Porlock, and Dunster: The Sea-board of Exmoor** With Map. By C. E. LARTER ... ... 1/- 6d.
19 **Cranbrook: The Town of the Kentish Weald.** Second Edition With Map. By STANLEY MARTIN ... ... 1/6 6d.
20 **Dawlish, and the Estuary of the Exe.** Cloth Edition contains Map. By BEATRIX F. CRESSWELL ... ... 1/- 6d.
21 **St. Albans: Its Abbey and its Surroundings.** With Map. By C. H. ASHDOWN, F.R.G.S., F.C.S. 2/6 1/-
22 **Bromley, Beckenham and Chislehurst.** By GEORGE CLINCH, F.G.S. With an Introduction by PHILIP NORMAN, F.S.A. With Map (1902) 2/6 1/-
23 **Exeter and its Cathedral.** By BEATRIX F. CRESSWELL. With Plan 1/- 6d.
24 **Kingston-upon-Thames and Surbiton.** With Map. By DR. W. E. ST. L. FINNY 2/6 1/-
25 **Evesham and its Neighbourhood, including Broadway.** With Map 1/6 1/-
26 **Petworth and Mid West Sussex.** With Map. (Cloth only.) ... 1/-
27 **Newquay, The Vale of Lanherne and Perranzabuloe.** By FANNIE GODDARD. With Map (1903) ... ... 1/- 6d.
28 **Haslemere and Hindhead.** By J. E. MORRIS, B.A. With Map (1903) 2/6 1/-
29 **Taunton and Taunton Deane.** By BEATRIX F. CRESSWELL. Map 2/6 1/-
30 **Littlehampton, Arundel and Amberley.** By REV. W. GOODLIFFE, M.A. Map (1903).... ... ... 1/- 6d.
31 **Tavistock. The Western Gate of Dartmoor.** By W. CROSSING. Map (1903). Introduction by REV. S. BARING-GOULD ... 1/- 6d.
32 **Plymouth. "The Metropolis of the West."** By W. H. K. WRIGHT. Map (1903). ... ... 1/- 6d.
33 **The Chalfont Country, South Bucks.** With Map. 1/6 1/-
34 **Dunstable, The Downs and the District.** With Maps. By G. WORTHINGTON SMITH, F.L.S., &c. 2/- 1/-
35 **The Quantock Hills** (Cloth only). With Map. By BEATRIX F. CRESSWELL 2/6 —
36 **Oxted, Limpsfield, and Edenbridge.** With Map. By GORDON HOME 1/- 6d.
37 **Lynton, Lynmouth, and The Lorna Doone Country.** With Map. By J. E. MORRIS, B.A. ... ... 1/- 6d.
38 **Horsham and Its Surroundings.** With Map. By REV. W. GOODLIFFE, M.A. 2/- 1/-
Week-Ends in Dickens' Land. With Map ... ... — 9d.
Week-Ends in Hop Land. With Map ... ... — 9d.

Handbooks for many other Towns and Districts are in active preparation.

LANTERN LECTURE.

MR. PRESCOTT ROW, Editor of the Homeland Handbooks, can accept Engagements for the following Lecture, fully illustrated, with original slides :—

Some Villages, Ancient Churches, and Historic Houses In North=West Kent.

Send for Prospectus.

For terms apply to PRESCOTT ROW,

The Homeland Association for The Encouragement of Touring in Great Britain.

ASSOCIATION HOUSE,   *Private Address—*
22, BRIDE LANE,   LITTLECOT,
FLEET STREET, E.C.   WADDON, SURREY.

The Homeland Library.

A SERIES of Local Histories by Expert Topographical Writers, handsomely bound for the Library uniform with this volume.

Vol. I.—Teignmouth : its History and Surroundings

by BEATRIX CRESSWELL, illustrated by Gordon Home.

A delightful book upon South Devon, principally dealing with the Estuary of the River Teign. Only one hundred copies now obtainable. 6/- net. Foolscap 4to.

"Miss Cresswell gossips pleasantly about the many features of interest. Teignmouth has literary associations of considerable importance. The illustrations throughout the book all by Mr. Gordon Home, of which there are a great number, are excellent, some of the landscapes are simply delightful. All lovers of the soft Devon scenery should buy the book."—*The Antiquary.*

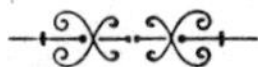

Vol. II.—Epsom : its History and Surroundings.

By GORDON HOME, illustrated by the Author, with an introduction by A.R. (The Right Hon. the Earl of Rosebery). Foolscap 4to. 6/- net. 194 pages, with 44 illustrations.

This book should be in the library of every lover of Surrey.

FROM A LEADER IN "THE STANDARD."

"Mr. Gordon Home's attractive volume on Epsom, just published by The Homeland Association, enjoys the advantage at least over most of the books of popular topography with which the press teems. It contains an introduction written by a distinguished resident, but since the classic little town no longer possesses many individuals who can be so described, and as the veiled sponsor signs the initials A,R., the authorship is no mystery. In any case internal evidence would point to Lord Rosebery as the author of these pages of graceful and rather mordant prose." *(Here follows half a column of description, and the notice concludes :)* "The spectacle of an ex Prime Minister diverting himself by writing a preface to a guide-book is unusual, but politicians who have held the highest offices in the State have been known to be worse employed, and the now popular study of local topography may innocently enough console the voluntary leisure of statesmen *en retraite.*"

Vol. III.—Dunstable : its History and Surroundings.

By WORTHINGTON G. SMITH, F.L.S., F.A.I., F.R.S.A., Ireland. Illustrated with drawings by the Author, and by photographs. Published in co-operation with the Corporation of Dunstable. Foolscap 4-to. 6/- net.

Vol. IV.—*In Preparation.*

The King's Homeland (Sandringham and North West Norfolk). By W. A. DUTT, author of "Highways and Byways in East Anglia," etc., with an introduction written by the desire of H.M. the King, by H. Rider Haggard.

This volume will describe the charming country round Sandringham, including Kings Lynn, Castle Rising, and Houghton.

The book will contain some beautiful illustrations, espccially painted by Mr. Gordon Home.

Foolscap 4-to. 6/- net. to be published in October, 1904.

A limited large paper edition will be issued at a price to be determined, probably 25/-.

Where to Shop at Dunstable.

A. ANDERSON & SON,

60, High Street North, Dunstable.

A few doors north of the Sugar Loaf Hotel. **Established 1869.**

Ladies' & Gentlemen's Tailors, Hatters, Hosiers, & Outfitters.

WE hold the Largest Stock of High-class SCOTCH and WEST OF ENGLAND TWEEDS, SUITINGS, and OVERCOATINGS in the District. All work is executed on the premises by experienced men under our personal supervision.

LIVERIES A SPECIALITY.

On receipt of a post card Mr. Anderson will call on gentlemen at their own residences.

We always have an up-to-date Stock of .

HATS, CAPS, TIES, GLOVES, &c.

Agents for—Dr. Jaeger's Sanitary Woollen Clothing, The Celebrated W Make 'Hat, Anderson's Waterproofs, I.H.S. and Prolis Raincoats, Lion Make Shirts and Collars.

A. ANDERSON & SON,

60, High Street North, DUNSTABLE